Paul Bélanger

Theories in Adult Learning and Education

Barbara Budrich Publishers
Opladen & Farmington Hills, MI 2011

A CIP catalogue record for this book is available from
Die Deutsche Bibliothek (The German Library)

ISBN 978-3-86649-362-9

Die Deutsche Bibliothek – CIP-Einheitsaufnahme
Ein Titeldatensatz für die Publikation ist bei Der Deutschen Bibliothek erhältlich.

Verlag Barbara Budrich Barbara Budrich Publishers
Stauffenbergstr. 7. D-51379 Leverkusen Opladen, Germany

28347 Ridgebrook. Farmington Hills, MI 48334. USA
www.barbara-budrich.net

Institutional Editor: University of Duisburg-Essen, Germany
Jacket illustration by disegno, Wuppertal, Germany – www.disenjo.de
Copy-editing: Carsten Bösel
Typeset by Susanne Albrecht, Germany – www.lektorat-albrecht.de
Printed in Europe on acid-free paper by
Books on Demand, Norderstedt

Contents

Preface

In the past, learning and education were considered to take place primarily during the first ten or fifteen years of people's lives. The practice of compulsory school education is especially illustrative of this traditional notion of education. At least since the second half of the 20th century, the number of years devoted mainly to education has grown in the Western world. In some countries, it is still not unusual for people pursuing a university degree to dedicate the first 30 years of their lives primarily to education. However, the emergence of information and knowledge-based societies has challenged this model. In a world of rapidly evolving knowledge, changing living environments, and ongoing changes at the workplace, it is evident that each member of society is asked to engage in learning and education throughout their entire life. The idea of "inventory learning" of initial stocktaking does not fit anymore. This outdated concept needs to be replaced with a notion of learning and education that is combined more closely with people's whole lives. Last but not least, current demographic developments require adults to keep engaging in learning activities instead of leaving the whole "learning burden" to a decreasing young generation.

It does not come as a surprise, therefore, that adult education has evolved into a field of practice and an academic discipline in its own right over recent decades. The general question whether adults are still able to learn or not is behind us now. Of course they are! Their ways of learning are different from those of school pupils, however. Nowadays, the whole world speaks about the importance of lifelong learning. This concept includes the idea that people are able to learn throughout their lives and at all locations, as long as they are somehow motivated to do so. As a field of practice, adult education provides learning opportunities for adults. As an academic discipline, adult education aims at researching the specific conditions that support or constrain adults' learning. What is specific about adult learning? How can adults be motivated to take part in adult learning and education?

When thinking about adult education as an academic discipline, these two questions – "How do adults learn?" and "Who participates in adult learning?" – emerge as the discipline's core questions. In the present volume of the Study Guides in Adult Education series, Paul Bélanger places these questions in an interdisciplinary framework that involves a number of neighbouring disciplines, especially psychology, sociology, and philosophy. In the first part of the book, he introduces readers to the three major learning theories of "behaviourism", "cognitivism", and "constructivism/socio-constructivism". Based on these fundamentals, he then goes on to present learning theories with a special focus on adult learning: "humanist theory", "experiential learning", and "transformative learning". In the second part of the book, the issue of participation in adult learning and education is addressed from both an empirical and an analytical point of view. With the help of recent empirical data, Bélanger illustrates the vast differences in adult education participation rates across various countries according to criteria such as age, gender, initial education, occupation, or firm size. Based on this data, he concludes with a lucid analysis of the current state of adult learning and education participation.

This study guide does not only offer an overview of adult learning and participation theories, however. It also provides exercises to help readers engage more deeply with the text. Furthermore, the study guide features a variety of tasks designed to point readers to important literature about individual topics, inviting them to study some of the original sources in adult learning and participation.

Sincere thanks go to Paul Bélanger for contributing to this study guide series. Warm thanks also go to Henning Pätzold for his collegial review. Paul Bélanger has written this book in the context of his guest professorship within the DAAD Guest Chair in "Adult and Continuing Education and Learning" at the University of Duisburg-Essen. Since being a guest professor in the summer of 2008, he has inspired us with his approach regarding the intimacy of lifelong learning: "learning is a socialisation process and the inner driven construction of one-self". Readers will find this ambiguity throughout the entire study guide.

Regina Egetenmeyer

1. Introduction

If Adult Learning and Education (ALE) is now a recognised professional field, its theoretical perspectives, underlying practices and policies draw on a variety of academic disciplines. Various learning theories and theories of adult education participation shape the practice and the "engineering" of activities in the dispersed field of adult learning.

This publication, designed as a student guide to accompany the seminar on "Theories in Adult Learning", aims to explore theories of adult learning and adult education participation, providing a frame of reference for understanding and eventually improving the development of this rapidly evolving field.

The review of the various learning theories will include the behaviourist, cognitive, constructivist approaches and their modern development as well as specific developments in adult education theory.

This publication also examines the different psychological and sociological theoretical backgrounds of adult education participation in order to understand factors at work in the various participation patterns along the adult life course and between different social contexts.

The publication is thus divided into two parts: **Part I** on adult learning theories and **Part II** on adult education participation theories.[1]

1 We acknowledge Magali Robitaille, who did the preliminary research on adult learning research theories.

Part One:
Adult Learning Theories

2. Introduction to Adult Learning Theories

What does it mean to learn? What goes on in our minds when we acquire or mobilise new knowledge and skills? How do different environments influence learning aspirations and learning processes? What is the significance of past experiences and of informal learning? How do we interpret *learning mistakes* and their impact? How do we apprehend the various roles of teachers, trainers, facilitators, or mentors? More generally, what are the main driving forces in the learning life course and the various possible sequences in learning biographies?

Diverse interpretations and responses have been given to these questions. Various learning theories have proposed specific concepts to grasp the complex reality of human learning. Among these learning theories attempting to capture and systematise the learning process and its specificities, three major orientations have emerged and continue to evolve: *behaviourist theory (Skinner, Thorndyke, Watson), *cognitivist (Brunner, Gagné) and socio-cognitivist theories (Bandura), and *constructivist (Dewey, Piaget, Vygotsky) and socio-constructivist (Lave and Wenger) theories. Reviewing the literature on the learning process, one could of course find a much broader variety of theoretical frameworks. For this introductory section, however, we decided to focus on these three founding theoretical approaches and their subsequent development.

Inspired by these analyses or their critical assessment, other learning theories have been developed that are closer to the specific contexts of adult learning. We will go on by exploring three of these approaches: *humanist learning theory (Rogers), *experiential learning theory (Kolb and Schön, further developed in the adult learning field by Jarvis and Illeris), and *transformative theory (Mezirow).

Figure 1: Learning theories and key authors

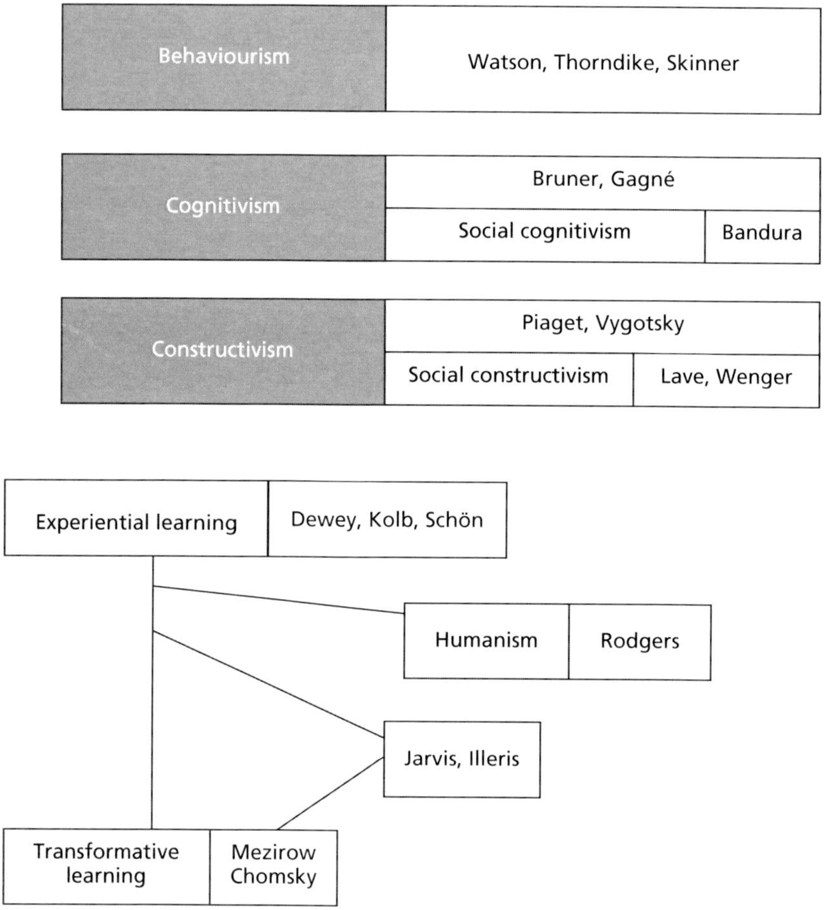

Source: Author's own

Exercises

Exercise 1

To learn is to increase our internal capacity to act and express ourselves. But then, how do we learn? Look at our own experience.

What went on when

- you, as a young girl or boy, kept trying to lace your shoes until, all of a sudden, you were finally able to do so?
- you gradually improved your English as a Second Language skills? How did you progressively acquire new vocabulary?
- you developed a curiosity for, say, the geography of Central Europe and progressively increased you knowledge about it?

Exercise 2

Reflecting on your educational life course, are there any specific conditions or contexts that, at some point, helped you to learn better or kept you from learning?

3. Three Main Learning Theories

The learning process is somewhat enigmatic and will probably remain a mystery to a certain extent. The truth is that multiple definitions of learning exist, as the process may be objectively observed from a wide range of disciplinary perspectives and with a variety of different objectives or concerns in mind. Moreover, the learning process is obviously complex. Each learning theory presented here contributes to our understanding of how people learn and the conditions under which they learn. As a consequence, there are overlapping and opposing views. Within the perspective of adult learning and lifelong learning, we will explore the richness of this scientific heritage as well as its contradictions.

3.1 Behaviourism

Behaviourism is the first theoretical orientation to emerge in the early years of the 20th century. It came out in reaction to the non-scientific or non-empirical and prescriptive analysis of learning which prevailed during that period.

It was developed initially by John B. Watson (Watson, 1930), widely known for his collaborative research on reflexes and conditioned responses with Russian physiologist Ivan Pavlov. Behaviourist researchers, challenging the prevalent trend in this early period of educational science, focused their studies on empirical and discernible behaviours rather than on "mental" processes.

Key concepts of behaviourism

- Contiguity
- Reinforcement
- Stimulus-response
- Operant conditioning
- Contingency

Their epistemological decision to keep these internal and hard-to-observe processes in a black box was critical, since, from their point of view, it was the only way of making sure their analyses would be truly empirical. Their attention, therefore, was concentrated on and limited to observable phenomena. "All we need to know to describe and explain behavior", wrote B.F. Skinner (1953), "is this: actions followed by good outcomes are likely to recur, and actions followed by bad outcomes are less likely to recur".

Textbox 1: Operating behaviour

"The process of operant conditioning (...) is simple enough. When a bit of behavior has the kind of consequence called reinforcing, it is more likely to occur again. A positive reinforcer strengthens any behavior that produces it (...). A negative reinforcer strengthens any behavior that reduces or terminates it. (...)The probability that a person will respond in a given way because of a history of operant reinforcement changes as the contingencies change(...) <however> the behavior is erroneously attributed to the feelings rather than to the contingencies responsible for what is felt".

Skinner, B. (1974). *About behaviorism.* New York: Knopf pp. 46 and 57

This theory of learning has often been reduced to Pavlov's well known experiments conditioning dogs. However, the learning process involved within such a perspective is much more complex, as is evident from the stimulus-response psychological framework.

The environment shapes behaviour and thus determines the learning process. Learning takes place through **reinforcement** when, in the course of repeating many contiguous events, the individual recurrently undergoes a rewarding experience. The **contiguity** of similar events in sequence could create a bond.

This stimulus-response theory of learning, explaining why behaviour patterns are strengthened by positive stimuli and weakened by negatives ones, was one of Thorndike's (Thorndike, 1931, 1932) contributions. In his laboratory of animal psychology, Thorndike observed that, through trial and error, animals select the more satisfying behaviour according to his famous **law of effect**. This law stipulates an increased probability of behaviour being repeated if it produces a better state of affairs. In other words, one will tend to acquire and remember a behaviour that has produced a positive effect. **Responses (R) to stimuli (S)** are reinforced by consecutive and consequent behaviour. Repeating gratifying behaviour tends to create lasting learned behaviour. However, for learning to proceed on the basis of repetition of meaningful effects, an organism should be ready for or in need of making such a connection.

Later, referring to the *Law of Effect* and the "effect of reinforcers", Skinner (1974) analyzed the operating condition, which determines the power of reinforcement, whether positive or negative. His work shows that since behaviour is learned, "it can be determined by arranging the contingencies of reinforcement in the learner's immediate environment" (Merriam & Caffarella, 1999, p. 252).

> The probability that a person will respond in a given way because of a history of operant reinforcement changes as the contingencies change. (…) When a given act is always reinforced, a person is said to have a feeling of confidence. (…) <However> the behavior is erroneously attributed to the feelings rather than to the contingencies responsible for what is felt. (Skinner, 1974, p. 57 ss.)

At a pedagogical level, behaviourists emphasise the importance of establishing gradual operational learning objectives, from simple to complex tasks, with a view to the predicted set of behavioural outcomes. "By systematically adjusting the stimuli throughout a course of study, the instructor can alter and fine-tune the behavior of the learners and modify the outcomes" (Leonard, 2002, p. 16).

Chart 1: Basic principles and pedagogical implications according to behaviourist learning theory

Epistemological orientation:	Learning is explained by combining the proper external conditions
Analytical units:	Observed behaviours Stimulus-response reinforcement
Forces that drive learning:	External social and material reinforcement
Learning situation, structure:	Highly structured situation Operant conditioning
Mistake status:	Learner's mistakes are a source of problems, not a learning experience. Mistakes have to be avoided.
Learning sequence:	Hierarchical sequence: from simple to complex, step by step.

Source: Chart adapted from Allal (1998) and Astolfi (1997).

> Educators using such a behaviorist framework preplan a curriculum by breaking a content area into assumed component parts –"skills" – and then sequencing these parts into a hierarchy ranging from simple to more complex.(...) This model makes the assumption that wholes can be broken into parts, and that these skills<and sub-skills>can be sequenced in a learning line. Learners are taught until (...) behavioral competence is achieved. (Fosnot, 2005)

However, the classic behaviourist approach, focusing on recognizable types of behaviour, tended to disregard internal cognitive and affective processes. The neo-behaviourist approach, which emerged later, did start to look at some affective or attitudinal variables, such as motivation and perseverance. These later modifications notwithstanding, the main assumption of behaviourist theory remains

> that instruction is achieved by observable, measurable, and controllable objectives set by the instructor and met by the learners who elicit a specific set of responses based upon a controlled set of stimuli. (...) Behaviorism does not concern itself with the learner's internal mental states, constructs, and symbols that cognitivism considers in its focus on learning process. (Leonard, 2002)

Focused on control and adaptive response, behaviourists ignore the subjective production of meanings; hence they limit its usefulness to situations where automatisms and immediate conformity are required.

Reference to this learning theory tends to be frequently made in some specific areas of activity where predicted specific behaviour is expected, e.g. in the field of publicity and marketing. In the domain of adult education and training, this approach continues to be used quite often in two specific areas at the workplace: health and safety training as well as quality control in production units.

Exercises and Tasks

Exercise 1

Could you identify typical education and training practices related to this theoretical perspective ("Reinforce desired behaviour and extinguish undesired behaviour")?

Exercise 2

In your own life experience, what type of learning did you achieve that could be interpreted within this framework?

Exercise 3

What parallels could you draw between behaviourist theory and some publicity strategies?

Task 1

B.F. Skinner, throughout the following text, is adamant on the importance of "probability of response". Referring to the full text, why do you think Skinner insists so much on this concept?
Skinner, B.F. (1950). Are theories of learning necessary? *Psychological Review* 57, 193–2316
http://psychclassics.yorku.ca/Skinner/Theories/

Task 2

In the following criticism of skinner's theory, Chomsky opposed his vision of "autonomous men" to a social world where "probabilities of response" are determinable. Could you explain why Chomsky is so critical of the concept of conditioning behaviour?
Chomsky, Noam (1971). The case against B.F. Skinner. *The New York Review of Books*, December 30.
http://www.ehu.es/HEB/KEPA/The%20Case%20Against%20B.F.%20Skinner.pdf

Note

It is always more rewarding to go back to the original sources. For an in-depth introduction to Skinner's behavourism, his two best-known books are highly recommended reading;

Skinner, B.F. (1953). *Science and human behavior.* New York: Macmillan.

Skinner, B.F. (1974). *About behaviorism.* New York: Knopf.

3.2 Cognitivism

What happens in the black box of the behaviourist approach? What goes on in the mind of a learner? Influenced by research on artificial intelligence, cognitivist theory interprets cognitive processes, such as reasoning, in terms of information handling and organisation (Legendre, 2005).

Textbox 2: The human condition of learning

"Is the animal trial-and-error prototype representative of human learning? The answer is clearly no. (...). If human beings are put in a problem box, we know that they are likely to adopt a strategy of searching for a way out. (...) They think out the consequences of their actions before they take them and choose the most likely alternative. Once they find their way out they are likely to remember the method (...)."

Gagné, R. (1985). *The conditions of learning and theory of instruction,* N.Y.: CBS Pub.

Cognitivist theory takes its cue from Gestalt theory, which interprets learning as an inner cognitive process. In contrast to behaviourists' search for general laws governing and predicting behaviour, cognitivists consider the so called "non-observable" cognitive process to be central for understanding learning processes. Overt behaviours tend to be ruled by such inner processes.

For the Gestaltist, learning is a cognitive phenomenon through which the learner thinks about all the elements required to solve a problem, eventually linking them together to grasp the situation. The learner is thus positioned at the centre of this inner process. The key concept, in Gestalt theory, is the occurrence of a sudden insight, this particular *Eureka*, the connect-the-dots moment when the learner comes to "see" relations and find solutions. The learning process proceeds through successive steps of trial and errors or experimentation, followed by insight and by formulating a solution, moving from **simple to complex** cognition. The next time, learners are able to reproduce the solution with less hesitation and finally develop or induce the underlying principle.

Cognitivist theory goes beyond external behaviour in order to understand what happens inside the learner's brain in all learning instances. Acquiring and processing knowledge is a cognitive process, a rational one. This information-processing theory relies on three key aspects of the learning process: memory, knowledge, and representation. Acquiring and processing knowledge is a mental process, through which the learner stores, orders, organises, transforms, retrieves, recovers, and evaluates **procedural** (know how) **and non-procedural knowledge**. It is the capacity to abstract a representation of facts or procedures that make knowledge transfer possible. The role of memory in such information processing is central and complex. **Long term memory** differs structurally and functionally from short term or working memory. In the retrieval of knowledge, information is initially registered in **short term memory** and then processed, transferred, and encoded into long term memory (LTM). In action, the competent learner retrieves pertinent codified information from his long term memory in order to generate relevant responses.

Textbox 3: Role of memory

"The stimulation that is constantly being received is organized into various patterns of neural activity, some of which are stored in the learners' memory in such a way that they can be recovered. Such memories may then be translated into action".

Gagné, R. (1985). *Ibid.*

Cognitive dissonance is a good example to illustrate the relevance of cognitivist concepts and pedagogical approaches. In a new context, perceiving an inconsistency among our cognitions generates a state of incertitude (dissonance), which motivates us to seek new consistency among our cognitions and the new piece of information. This "cognitive theory with an engine", as Gerard (1992) defined cognitive dissonance, helps to understand the emotional dimension of learning and the inner workings of the affective and cognitive processes involved.

Knowledge could not be acquired and processed, nor could it be transferred across situations, without being extracted from its life context and then transmitted. It is the capacity to abstract a representation of facts or procedures that makes knowledge transfer possible. Though verbal expression tends to precede reflection, it remains a systematic and rational way through which the learner perceives cognitive procedures and schemas.

Key concepts of the cognitivist approach

- Procedural (know how) and non-procedural knowledge
- Short and long term memory
- Knowledge transfer
- Metacognition
- Cognitive dissonance
- Simple to complex learning sequence

Talking, reflecting, and knowing about such processes is a key element of the cognitivist analysis, referred to as the concept of metacognition. Metacognition is the extent to which the learner is conscious of his or her learning processes and knowledge. This conscious knowledge about one's own cognition is a key factor in any learning process.

Chart 2: Basic principles and pedagogical implications according to cognitivist learning theory

Epistemological orientation:	Learning is explained by internal processes confronted with external conditions.
Analytical units:	Cognitive processes and *observable* results, Learner's representations, strategies, and procedures
Forces that drive learning:	Cognitive conflict, problem situations
Learning situation, structure:	Open situations permitting discovery and exploration
Mistake status:	Learner's mistakes are a source of learning, because they generate cognitive conflict
Learning sequence:	Spiral sequence: from complex to simple to complex again

Source: Chart adapted from Allal (1998) and Astolfi (1997).

Bruner (1996, 2009), reflecting on how the mind works, does not deny the existence of some parallels between human learning processes and the kind of information processing performed by computational devices. He insists, however, that the mind of an individual always operates in a specific cultural setting which has an influence both on the subjective production of meanings and the internal organisation of information. For such information processing to take place, individuals not only need instrumental tools, but also a cultural context in which they can receive feedback and experience cultural exchange.

Bandura (1977, 1994) expanded the cognitivist approach by integrating the social perspective in his analysis of learning processes, i.e. the interdependence of personal and environmental influences. Even though positioning the learner at the centre of the learning process, Bandura reminds us of the reciprocal interaction between individuals and their milieu:

> For the most part, the environment is only a potentiality until actualized by appropriate actions (...). Similarly, personal determinants are only potentialities that do not operate as influences unless they are activated. (...) Thus, behavior partly determines which of the many potential environmental influences will come into play and what forms they will take; environmental influences, in turn, partly determine which behavioral repertoires are developed and activated. In this two-way influence process, the environment is influenceable, as is the behavior it regulates. (Bandura, 1977, p. 195)

Social interactions influence behaviour.

If people's beliefs or judgments about their own capabilities play a key role in any learning process, such perceived self-efficacy is reciprocally influenced by an individual's life-story and by his or her current life and work context.

> Intellectual development is multifaceted and encompasses different types of abilities that vary in how heavily they draw on such component cognitive processes as attention, memory, time-sharing, information integration, and level of knowledge and expertise. Cognitive functioning is multi-directional, following different trajectories of change for different abilities. Some improve, others remain stable, and still others decline with age. (Bandura, 1994, p. 199)

Human development is a lifelong process. Each period of life presents learning demands requiring the ongoing development of personal efficacy for successful participation in society. However, pejorative stereotypes may shape cultural expectations and evaluative reactions of inefficacy toward discriminated groups such as the elderly. Undermined belief in one's ability and weakened self-efficiency may seriously impair the autonomous pursuit of a learning biography.

Competency, in that perspective, is seen as a mix of tacit and codified knowledge. Focusing on the processing and transmission of knowledge, the contribution of the cognitivist approach is highly relevant in designing learning proposals that build on people's existing information background and knowledge. The notion of "learning to learn" within a lifelong vision of learning could not be dissociated from the notion of metacognition.

Learning, however, is more than a mental retrieval process governing the learner's actions. It is the reflexive act of a subject. In a situation where people experience inconsistency between personal belief or acquired knowledge and new belief or ideas, they tend to reduce this dissonance either by changing their attitudes, beliefs, and behaviours, or by justifying and rationalising their own conviction and prior knowledge. Significant learning takes place through such deconstruction and reconstruction of one's representation and through such mobilisation of new knowledge. Curiosity and openness to challenges are important factors helping people improve their capacity to act and reinforce their autonomy. Here, important limitations of the cognitivist approach become evident. It tends to disregard the importance of reflexivity and the level of self-awareness acquired by learners. For learners, becoming aware of their learning process in their specific context is indeed a critical ability which could predict their autonomy and self-development throughout their life course (see, for example, Fagan (1988) on the role of metacognition in adult literacy).

Exercises and Tasks

Exercise 1

Can you give concrete examples of *typical adult cognitive skills, *creative thinking outside the deduction process, and *cognitive dissonance?

Exercise 2

Discuss the concept of metacognition in the context of adult literacy.

Exercise 3

In a cement factory, the mechanic is used to repair the special water system in trucks. When problems occur, he is sure to find a solution. However, he cannot explain the way he proceeds to detect and solve the problem. He has difficulty transferring his expertise. His attempt to explain could not be understood by his or her co-workers. Discuss the situation using the concepts of tacit and explicit knowledge, and of procedural and non-procedural knowledge.

Task 1

In the text mentioned below, Gagné explains that there is no magic in learning. It is a development process involving memory and transfer. By combining and transferring previously acquired knowledge, the learner cumulates expertise. Considering the domain of adult literacy or numeracy, could you explain Gagné's vision of a cumulative learning sequence?

Gagné, R. (1985). *The conditions of learning and theory of instruction* (4th ed.). New York: CBS College Publishing. Chapter 1, pages 37-60. http://www.ibstpi.org/Products/pdf/chapter_1.pdf

Task 2

In the text below, Bandura explores the social dimension of learning processes and hence the relative determinants of life paths. As an example, he points to the gender stereotypes that people adopt and that often have lasting effects. Could you explain, in such a case, how people perceive and process past experiences and how they could use their capabilities and their environment to pilot and possibly rectify their personal development?

Bandura, A. (1989). Social cognitive theory. In R. Vasta (Ed.), *Annals of child development. Vol.6. Six theories of child development* (pp. 1-60). Greenwich, CT: JAI Press.
http://www.decolonizing.com/pdfs/Bandura%20%281989%29.pdf

See also Bruner, J. S. (1965). The growth of mind. *American Psychologist*, 20, 1007-1017.

3.3 Constructivism and socio-constructivism

Constructivism

The constructivist orientation highlights the fact that learners must actively construct their knowledge. "Basically, a constructivist stance maintains that learning is a process of constructing meaning; it is how people make sense of their experience" (Merriam & Caffarella, 1999, p. 261).

Constructivism is a poststructuralist psychological theory (...), one that construes learning as an interpretive, recursive, nonlinear building process by active learners interacting with their surrounding – the physical and social world. It is a psychological theory of learning that describes how structures, language, activity, and meaning-making come about, rather

> than one that simply characterizes the structures and stages of thought, or one that isolates behaviors learned through reinforcement. It is a theory based on complexity models of evolution and development. (Fosnot, 2005, p. 291)

Learning is an **internal progressive** cognitive process through which an individual, confronted by a new environment or new knowledge, recurrently modifies his/her knowledge or **learning scheme**, thereby **constructing** new **meaning.** Teaching, from a personal constructivism perspective, involves providing

> experiences that induce cognitive conflict and hence encourage learners to develop new knowledge schemes that are better adapted to experience. Practical activities supported by group discussions form the core of such pedagogical practices. (Driver et al., 1994, p. 6; as cited in Merriam & Caffarella, 1999, p. 262)

A key aspect of constructivism is cognitive conflict, which is described as a vector of learning. Within the constructivist paradigm, "learning is a self-regulating process" when facing a disturbing or unfamiliar situation.

> Teaching and learning, especially for adults, is a process of negotiation, involving the construction and exchange of personally relevant and viable meanings (…). A constructivist perspective is congruent with much of adult learning theory.
> (Merriam & Caffarella, 1999, p. 262)

> The constructivist view of learning is particularly compatible with the notion of self-direction, since it emphasizes the combined characteristics of active inquiry, independence, and individuality in a learning task. (Candy, P., as cited in Merriam & Caffarella, 1999, p. 262-263)

It was Dewey (1940) who brought up the importance of contextualisation. Knowledge must be constructed in a significant context if we expect people to mobilise it and eventually transfer it to other life contexts. "I believe", wrote Dewey,

> that the individual who is to be educated is a social individual, and that society is an organic union of individuals. If we eliminate the social factor from the child we are left only with an abstraction; if we eliminate the individual factor from society, we are left only with an inert and lifeless mass. Education, therefore, must begin with a psychological insight into the child's capacities, interests, and habits. It must be controlled at every point by reference to these same considerations. These powers, interests, and habits must be continually interpreted – we must know what they mean. They must be translated into terms of their social equivalents – into terms of what they are capable of in the way of social service. (1940, p. 6)

The concept of **situated cognition** was developed partly in response to the possible impact of compulsory school attendance, whereby the idiosyncratic experience of each learner tends to be ignored. Because cognition happens in context, it is important to ensure that teaching takes place in a context that makes sense in and for the learner's social life. The authenticity of the teaching context will help learners use their newly acquired knowledge in more general ways afterwards (Cordova & Lepper, 1996).

> Three main practical implications could be derived from the constructivist theoretical approach: a) priority should be given to the development of meaning and understanding rather than to behavioural training, b) researchers and teachers should presume that learners' actions and reactions are rational, considering how learners give meaning to their reality, c) learners' errors and unexpected responses should be interpreted as opportunities to know how they are grasping reality. (Legendre, 2005, p. 290, our translation)

Piaget's positions could be called constructivist in the sense that they underline the active and structuring role of learners and the importance of their conceptual schemes in building their knowledge and reality. According to Piaget's theory, children construct or adapt their cognitive structures and concepts in response to demands within their environment, thus progressively developing their identity. As explained by Piaget, they do so by going through four successive stages of intellectual and emotional development: sensorimotor stage (0-2 years old), preoperational stage (2-7 years), concrete operations stage (7-11 years), and formal operations stage (11-15 years) (Piaget, 1964).

Socio-constructivism

Knowledge acquisition and mobilisation are the result of an active construction and thinking process. The social constructivist view posits that knowledge is built when people engage socially in conversation and action on shared projects or problems. Within this approach, learning could not be isolated from the culturally shared ways of understanding and talking about the world and reality (Merriam & Caffarella, 1999, p. 262).

In that perspective, one of Vygotsky's important contributions to learning theory is the concept of "proximal development zone". The idea is to asses a learner's level of development and knowledge in order to create a learning situation that is beyond his or her actual level, but at the same time not too challenging so as to provoke failure. In that case, the learning situation remains within the "proximal development zone" of this person at this moment. The idea is to confront the learner with a learning situation or problem that is hard and complex enough to be challenging but not too difficult and hence discouraging. The purpose is to find a zone of development within which the learner can receive support and, as a result, achieve something that he or she would have been incapable of achieving all by themselves. The objective is to put learners in a context that enables them to mobilise their prior knowledge, confronting it with other realities and critical perceptions in order to overcome the disequilibrium that such a context creates.

Mediation of the psychological processes is the central fact of Vygotsky's conception; socially elaborated systems of signs are the means of mediation; these allow a control of the processes of behavior. Internalization and sociogenesis, which derive directly from this conception, are two inseparable aspects of the same process of construction of the different psychological capacities; on a certain level of development, they lead to a quasi-social behavior of the subject towards himself. The differentiation of functions is the main form of construction of new capacities: the analyses of the development of language are a good illustration of this principle. (Schneuwly, 1986, p. 16)

Another major contribution by Vygotsky is the related concept of "scaffolding". To be effective, the tutor must give an appropriate amount of support to learners. First, the tutor assesses learners' current level of knowledge and skills with regard to a particular situation. Subsequently, he adapts his support to meet the needs of each learner, who may then work inside their proximal development zone. Consequently, in certain situations, the tutor may give a lot of support to allow the learner to get involved in a difficult learning process. However, with time and practice, such support must eventually be phased out, enabling the leaner to become autonomous in dealing with this type of issue.

Chart 3: Basic principles and pedagogical implications according to social constructivism

Epistemological orientation:	Learning is explained by internal processes, but the emphasis is on social mediation; learning is contextualised
Analytical units:	Cognitive processes, social interaction processes, and acknowledgeable results Learner's regulations, representations, strategies and procedures
Forces that drive learning:	Social cognitive conflict, problem situations and the notion of proximal development zone
Learning situation, structure:	Open situations permitting discovery and exploration Scaffolding (teacher or peer interventions)
Mistake status:	Learner's mistakes are a source of learning, because they generate cognitive conflict Social confrontations, interactive regulations as source of social cognitive conflict
Learning sequence:	Spiral sequence: from complex to simple to complex again The sequence takes place in a relevant context

Source: Adapted from Allal (1998) and Astolfi (1997).

Refuting the individualist view of the learning process, Lave and Wenger (1991) look at learning as a "legitimate, peripheral participation in communities of practices". They always situate a learning event in the context of people's experience and of their specific participation in the world around them. From an anthropological point of view, Lave and Wenger observed tailor workshops in traditional Africa, studied butcher apprentices in a food store, and even examined the mathematical mental activity of people shopping and walking up and down the aisles in a grocery store. Based on these empirical observations, they discover and conceptualise how people develop and mobilise knowledge in relation to a specific context that is more or less conducive to such development. Moreover, they study how people, in such communities of action, involve themselves gradually (or are hindered to do so) with the idea of becoming competent actors, tailors, butchers, or consumers.

Lave's contribution (1993) is precisely her effort to conceptualise the dynamic relations between the actors and the social world. She mentions four premises regarding knowledge and learning: a) knowledge always undergoes construction and transformation, b) learning is an integral aspect of human activity, c) what is learned is always problematic, and d) acquisition of knowledge is not simply a matter of absorbing it, it requires personal search for pertinence and then mobilisation of such knowledge in the immediate context. The learning process, therefore, always takes place in "situated activities". The construction of professional and personal identities within a community of practice, as Wenger (1998) would say, is not a mere passive socialisation process, but an active and interactive one.

Key concepts of the constructivist approach:

- Central role of the learner (person acting) in his/her context
- Cognitive conflict, contradiction, and resolution of dilemma
- Reflective practice and abstraction
- Self-organisation and internal restructuring
- Proximal development zone (PDZ)
- Learning as an interactive process between subjective construction and external structure

Additional concepts of the socio-constructivist approach:

- Situated learning
- Social mediation, dialogue, interaction
- Dialectics between the subject AND the socio-cultural structure, between the acting person AND the constituted order
- Community of practices
- Peripheral legitimate participation
- Holistic approaches: the cognitive, conative and psycho-motor resources mobilised by the person in her action context
- Interactive process between subject and his context

The subject, experiencing a conflict between his current personal knowledge and meanings on the one hand and external new knowledge (or facts and observed action) on the other, will tend to question his current apprehension and will construct, out of this tension, a new synthesis. The way in which a person, in her context, resolves the dilemma brought on by cognitive conflict is, for Lave, a **dialectical process** between the person acting and the context (arena and settings). The synthesis, thus constructed by the acting person, will hold until the next cognitive conflict occurs. If the conflict is not too difficult, if the gap is not too wide – that is to say if it stays within his/her *proximal development zone* – it will stir a similar but higher-level dialectic process leading to a new, higher-level synthesis, which, again, is only temporary in nature, however.

In this interactive learning process, the driving force is not accommodation to change, but the cognitive conflict, the dilemma provisionally resolved through self-reorganisation. At the core of any learning process, one will observe a self-assertive tendency of the subject to act *in* and *on* his life or work context.

The lifelong learning sequence is seen as a spiral process whereby the learner, an active agent, is constructing him/herself, continuously reorganising his/her knowledge and meanings, deepening his/her interest and curiosity.

Socio-constructivism carries a critique of the notion of **knowledge transfer** and of the socialisation and functionalist view of learning put forth by cognitivist theory. According to constructivist theories, learners, while interacting with an environment, build their own mental structures. The pedagogical focus is task-oriented; it takes into account and even structures the learning environments where learners are invited to take initiatives and carry out self-directed tasks.

This theoretical framework re-positions learners in their respective contexts and provides tools for understanding how an individual is engaged in a self-constructing process throughout his/her life course. However, this approach tends to disregard the constituted procedural and nonprocedural knowledge which has to be grasped and well retrieved in one's mind in order precisely to strengthen the autonomy of the subject.

Exercises and Tasks

Exercise 1

Give and explain an example of cognitive conflict and its relevance in the learning process.

Exercise 2

Consider Piaget's four stages in the cognitive development of children: sensorimotor, pre-operation, concrete operational, and formal operational (see above). How do you see the further cognitive development along the adult life? Why do many adults hardly reach level 4?

Exercise 3

How and why do constructivists and socio-constructivists criticise the cognitivist notion of knowledge transfer?

Exercise 4

Referring to the notion of holistic learning process, socio-constructivist theory differentiates the cognitive, conative and psycho-motor resources mobilised by a person in his/her action context. Could you give examples of instances in which each of these three resources is mobilised and point out a few links between them?

Task 1

Constructivism is not a theory of teaching but a theory of learning. Referring to Fosnot, explain how this theory nevertheless has important implications for teaching practice.

Fosnot, C. T. (2005). Constructivism revisited: Implications and reflections. In C.T. Fosnot (Ed.), *Constructivism: Theory, perspectives, and practice* (pp. 276-291). New York: Teachers College Press.
http://www.odu.edu/educ/act/journal/vol16no1/fosnot.pdf

Task 2

For Lave, knowledge mobilisation could not be understood outside the context in which it takes place. Why, in her text below, does Lave consider this perspective to be so fundamental?

Lave, J. (1991). Situating learning in communities of practice. In L. B. Resnick, J.M. Levine & S.D. Teasley (Eds.), *Perspectives on socially shared cognition* (pp. 63-84). Washington, DC: American Psychological Association. http://www.udel.edu/educ/whitson/files/Lave,%20Situating%20learning%20in%20communities%20of%20practice.pdf

Note

See also Piaget, J. (1964). Development and Learning. *Journal of Research in Science Teaching*, 2, 176-186.
http://www.psy.cmu.edu/~siegler/piaget64.pdf

4. Adult Learning-related Learning Theories

Adult learning theorists such as Illeris, Knowles, Jarvis, Mezirow, and Tenant have increasingly made important contributions to general theories of learning over the last three decades. Concepts such as cognitive dissonance, situated learning, reflective practice, learning environment, transformative learning, and communities of practice are found in both adult learning and general education literature.

Within the three classical schools of thought presented in the previous sections, researchers have developed learning theories related to the specific domain of adult learning, addressing the following questions: Is the process of adult learning characterised by specific features? What are the main driving forces in adult learning? How do learning processes evolve over an individual's life course?

4.1 Humanist theory of adult learning

In the 1960s and 1970s, two specialists, both of them therapists and educators, Abraham Maslow, well-known for his "hierarchy of needs", and Carl Rogers, famous for his work on the personal relationship between facilitator and learner, developed the **humanist theory** of learning.

> From a learning theory perspective, humanism emphasizes that perceptions are centered in experience, as well as the freedom and responsibility to become what one is capable of becoming. These tenets underlie much of adult learning theory that stresses the self-directedness of adults and the value of experience in the learning process. (Merriam & Caffarella, 1999, p. 257)

The founder of humanistic psychology, Abraham Maslow (1970), proposed a theory of human motivation centred on a hierarchy of human needs, ranging from physiological needs at the lowest level to self-esteem and the need for self-actualisation at the highest level. According to this author, learning is a process through which people attempt to fulfill their individual potential; learning is a form of self-actualisation.

The fundamental question raised by therapist and educator Carl Rogers is, from a therapeutic perspective, not how to cure but how to build an authentic relationship between the therapist and the person. Similarly, from an educational perspective, the basic question is not how to teach, but how to build a relationship which the learner can use for his or her own personal growth in order to actualise him/herself.

> Human beings can control their own destiny; people are inherently good and will strive for a better world; people are free to act, and behavior is the consequence of human choice; people possess unlimited potential for growth and development. (Rogers, 1983, as cited in Merriam & Caffarella, 1999, p. 256)

Rogers abstracted ten principles from his experience in education settings and in his clinical work:

1) Human beings have a natural potentiality for learning.
2) Significant learning takes place when the subject matter is perceived by the student as having relevance for his overt purposes.
3) Learning which involves a change in self-organisation – in the perception of oneself – is threatening and tends to be resisted.
4) Those learnings which are threatening to the self are more easily perceived and assimilated when external threats are at a minimum.
5) When threat to the self is low, experience can be perceived in differentiated fashion and learning can proceed.
6) Much significant learning is acquired through doing.
7) Learning is facilitated when the student participates responsibly in the learning process.
8) Self-initiated learning which involves the whole person of the learner – feelings as well as intellect – are the most lasting and pervasive.
9) Independence, creativity, and self-reliance are all facilitated when self-criticism and self-evaluation are basic and evaluation by others is of secondary importance.
10) The most socially useful learning in the modern world is the learning of the process of learning, a continuing openness to experience and incorporation into oneself of the process of change. (Rogers, 1969, pp. 157ss)

Humanist theorists take a stand against many of the behaviourist conceptions, e.g. regarding their view of human nature, the conditioning of responses to stimuli, and "the notion that behavior is predetermined by either the environment or one's subconscious" (Merriam & Caffarella, 1999, p. 256). This vision of learning, inspired by psychological findings, sees the integral development of the individual as the finality of education. According to this perspective, the teacher is a facilitator seeking to actualise the learner's potential. The learner is the main agency of the process.

> The humanist approach could be seen as a natural continuation of the rationalist approach. Within this view, the subject is at the centre of the process and of the discourse; he is the agency of knowledge acquisition and appropriation. (Legendre, 2005, p. 741, our translation and adaptation)

Humanists analyze and interpret learning processes within a wider frame of reference, taking into account the **affective** as well as **cognitive** aspects of learning, considering the whole person, their feelings and intellect. Among the many dimensions influencing learning processes, humanists underline the roles of anxiety, the subconscious, repression, defense mechanisms, inner drive (libido), and 'coup manqué' (Freud). While putting forward a Freudian (psycho) analysis, they refuse to accept a deterministic vision of the subconscious. They have an **optimistic view** of people's inner capacity for growth, personal development, and change. For them, it is of primary importance to help individuals discover and valorise their capacity to grow and to change. **Learning, understood this way, is always ambivalent**: searching for one's identity, questioning one's beliefs, meanings or experiences, venturing into the unknown, and changing one's self-organisation may be frightening and threatening to the self.

Key concepts of humanist theory

Self-actualisation: the inner drive to extend, to expand, to activate one's capacity, to become autonomous, to develop, to mature, to enhance the self. The tendency for *self-actualisation* is universal, though often *latent*, hidden.

Learning experiences: the accumulated lived situations integrated by the individual through reflective practice.

Significant learning: learning becomes significant and thus sustainable when the experience is relevant, progressive, stimulant, and inner-directed.

A learning experience is **significant** when it has subjective meaning for the individual, i.e. when the individual can relate this learning event to their former experience and to their present context and needs. It is **progressive** when the individual can see that they are getting something out of it, enhancing their knowledge or their capacity for action, thus continuing to construct themselves. The learning experience is **stimulant** when the knowledge imparted and received addresses a personal question or answers some curiosity (personally meaningful learning). It is **inner-directed** when the individual has the feeling that they have achieved something all by themselves, that they have increased their inner capacity for action or expression, thus reinforcing their autonomy.

Role of the facilitator

The facilitator needs to be 'other person-centred' in order to develop an authentic relationship, to free and unleash curiosity, to raise questions, and to help people explore the unknown. This kind of facilitator-learner relationship implies

- **genuineness**, i.e. a transparent, true relationship including the expression of feelings,
- **acceptance** of the other as they are, recognising the value and potential of that person,
- **empathy**, i.e. sensitivity towards the other, making them free to explore new territory without fear of failure.

> In education, humanism focuses on the instructor's ability to foster the student's self-concept, autonomy, and ability to make personal decisions, as well as to be self-directed and ultimately self-learned. As such, humanism as an educational theory is allied to Linderman's views of adult education, Anderson's views of andragogy, and the discovery learning theory of Bruner, all of whom are constructivists. (Leonard, 2002, p. 86)

Rogers (1969, p. 164-166) uses ten main ideas to summarise his views on facilitator methods and qualities:

1. The facilitator has much to do with setting the initial mood or climate of the group or class experience (…),
2. The facilitator helps to elicit and clarify the purposes of the individuals in the class as well as the more general purposes of the group (…),
3. He relies upon the desire of each student to implement those purposes which have meaning for him, as the motivational force behind significant learning,
4. He endeavours to organise and make easily available the widest possible range of resources for learning,
5. He regards himself as a flexible resource to be utilised by the group,
6. In responding to expressions in the classroom group, he accepts both the intellectual content and the emotionalised attitudes, endeavouring to give each aspect the approximate degree of emphasis which it has for the individual or the group,

7. As the acceptant classroom climate becomes established, the facilitator is able increasingly to become a participant learner, a member of the group, expressing his views as those of one individual only,
8. He takes the initiative in sharing himself with the group – his feelings as well as his thoughts – in ways which do not demand nor impose but represent simply a personal sharing which students may take or leave,
9. Throughout the classroom experience, he remains alert to the expressions indicative of deep or strong feelings,
10. In his functioning as a facilitator of learning, the leader endeavors to recognise and accept his own limitations.

Hence, the key dimension of the humanist approach is to support learners' development and autonomy, keeping in mind their full potential and learning capacities.

> Human thinking and learning are driven by the growth of the self as a whole, mature, and complete human being, who has a strong character and an ability to make decisions that positively influence others. Humanism is completely concerned with inner self-actualization and individual transformation that occurs as a result of emotional and aesthetic responses to learning experiences. Humanism is concerned with the learner's self-direction, inner motivation, self-regulation, and personal growth that results from the learning process. (Leonard, 2002, p. 86)

Exercises and Tasks

Exercise 1

Could you give and discuss an example in which the same objective learning event could be **significant** for one learner but not for another?

Exercise 2

When Carl Rogers insists on the importance of the educator being 'other person-centred', what does he mean? Could you give counter examples?

Exercise 3

Why do you think Rogers insists so much on the ambivalence of learning, on the frightening search for one's identity, of venturing into the unknown, and of learning as a possible threat to the self?

Task 1

According to Rogers, in which kind of environment do people tend to learn more significantly?

Rogers, C. (1979). The foundations of the person-centered approach. *Education, 100,* 96–107. http://www.if-development.co.uk/Facilitation/Person%20centered%20approach.pdf

Task 2

In the document below about one of the key andragogists, Malcom Knowles, M.K. Smith shows how influential the notion of *relationships*, derived from humanistic clinical psychology, and the notion of *facilitator*, argued for by Carl Rogers, have been in adult learning. How does Smith relate these two notions to one another?

Smith, M. K. (2002). Malcolm Knowles, informal adult education, self-direction and anadragogy. In *The Encyclopedia of Informal Education.* www.infed.org/thinkers/et-knowl.htm.

4.2 Experiential learning

Experiential learning theory views learning as a "process by which knowledge is created and significant learning occurs through the transformation of one's experience and in reference to it". It "refers to a learner-centred approach whereby learners' past experiences provide, through induction, a meaningful reference for further learning. In that perspective, active learning becomes significant when related to real personal experience" (Legendre, 2005, p. 853, our translation and adaptation).

Key concept: Reflective practice

- Based on experience and prior (tacit and explicit) knowledge
- Focused on problem definition (discovering + revisiting) and problem solving
- Making judgment on action to be taken
- Action oriented, deliberate action

The first step in an experiential learning process is obviously an action or a condition viewed or registered subjectively. Then, the learner reflects on his action or experience in order to finally reinvest acquired knowledge and know-how in actions to come. According to this theory of learning, experience is the initial force that drives learning. To transform this experience into knowledge in a learning process, however, learners need to practise a reflexive attitude towards their actions and experiences.

Not all experiences lead to learning, of course. In the early 1970s, Kolb devised a cyclical model based on consecutive steps to better understand how individuals learn from their experience. He defines learning as "the process whereby knowledge is created through the transformation of experience", with knowledge resulting from "the combination of grasping and transforming experience" (Kolb, 1984, p. 41).

Again, "if all genuine education comes about through experience, not all experience educates" (Dewey, 1940). What is required is continuity plus **interaction** with the environment. Reflexive practice is one of the key concepts developed by Schön (1983). There is still a debate whether Schön actually meant reflecting on action or reflecting in action or both. The fact is that reflexive practice requires learners or practitioners to become conscious of their patterns of action and their ongoing conceptualisation. They must become able to analyze these patterns and explore their subjective and objective relevance.

Figure 2: Experiential Learning Cycle (ELC)

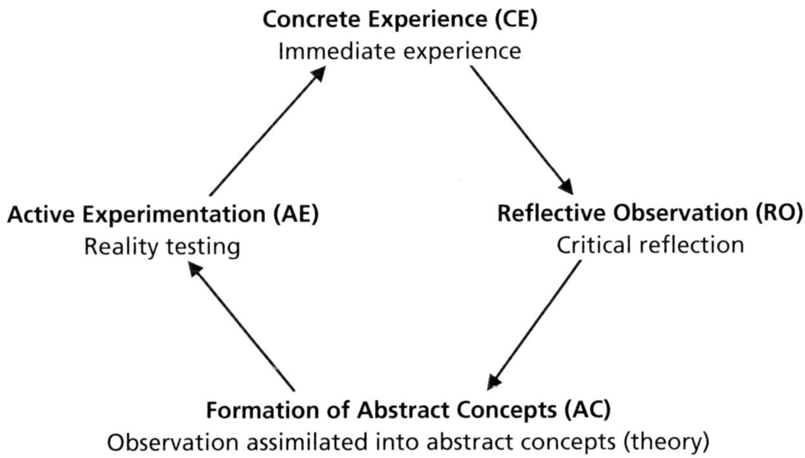

Source: Kolb, 1984, p. 141

Key concepts of Kolb's Experiential Learning Theory (ELT):

- Learner-centred
- Key role of experience in learning life course
- Learning is, initially, an inductive process
- Experience is turned into learning through reflection
- Spiral learning
- Experience-based learning system
- Autonomy-adaptation

Observing that cognition and learning are inextricably linked to context, experiential learning theorists, along with socio-constructivists, refer to the notions of **situated** or **embodied cognition**. Indeed, in real life, action and reflection are not two totally distinct aspects and phases of experience, since each pole of this relation informs the other, in the same way that theory enlightens practice and that practice inspires theoretical thinking. Like Kurt Lewin, the founder of the T-Group training method, used to say, "there is nothing so practical as a good theory".

Linking the two perspectives and recalling the relations between individuals and their environment as well as between subjects and their worlds, Peter Jarvis, one of the best known international researchers in adult learning, criticises Kolb's learning cycle for omitting the social and interactive dimensions. Jarvis defines learning in the following manner:

> Human learning is the combination of processes throughout a lifetime whereby the whole person (…) experiences social situations, the perceived content of which is then transformed cognitively, emotively or practically (or through any combination) and integrated into the individual person's biography resulting in a continually changing (or more experienced) person. (Jarvis, 2009, p. 25)

Experiential learning theory tends to favour approaches such as case studies, role playing, and, more broadly, content presentations that feature or enable references to significant and concrete learning situations. With its emphasis on context, biography, and real-life learning, this theory has resonated strongly with adult educators, since adult learners typically bring a lot of life experience to teaching-learning situations, seeking to integrate their previous related informal learning.

Exercises and Tasks

Exercise 1

How do case studies, role-playing, oral history, and life stories relate to experiential learning theory? Could you name a few other similar approaches?

Exercise 2

What are the strengths and limitations of experiential learning?

Exercise 3

Do you see any links between Kolb's and Rogers' frames of reference?

Task

Kelly, exploring the use of experiential learning theory in second language education, observes advantages and certain limits. Could you notice and assess in your own experience of ESL?

Kelly, C. (1997). David Kolb, The Theory of Experiential Learning and ESL. *The Internet TESL Journal*, Vol. III, No. 9, September 1997. Retrieved from http://iteslj.org/Articles/Kelly-Experiential/

Note

See also the following references:

Silberman, M. (2007). *The handbook of experiential learning.* San Francisco: Pfeiffer.

Beard, C. & Wilson, J. (2006). *Experiential learning. A best practice handbook for educators and trainers.* (2nd ed.). London/Philadelphia: Kogan Page. Extract 14: Chap. 2 (pp. 15-19).

Kolb, D. A., Boyatzis, R. & Mainemelis, C. (2001). Experiential learning theory: Previous research and new directions. In R.J. Sternberg & L.F. Zhang, (Eds.), *Perspectives on thinking, learning, and cognitive styles* (pp. 227–247). Mahwah, NJ: Lawrence Erlbaum.
http://www.learningfromexperience.com/images/uploads/experiential-learning-theory.pdf

4.3 Transformative learning

"The issue is not only to acquire new knowledge, but to develop new glasses to look differently at reality and existing knowledge". (Mezirow, 1991)

"The action and reflection of men (and women) upon their world in order to transform it". (Freire, 1973)

Mezirow

In the early 1980s, Jack Mezirow introduced the notion of transformative change into the analysis and interpretation of adult learning processes, which lead him to develop his theory of **transformative learning**. Together with Paolo Freire (1970), he raised an important question: if learning is about change and if learning *is* change, should we not consider different levels of personal and social changes?

The learning process may remain at an adaptive level by simply adding new knowledge and acquiring new skills, or it may lead to a transformation of the ways in which people look at their reality. In such a case, learning is not only concerned with seeing more things, but with seeing them differently. There is a critical difference between an assimilation process, in which new experiences are shaped to conform to an existing knowledge structure, and a transformative process, in which the knowledge structure itself is being changed. It is the difference between changes in *what*_we know and changes in *how*_we know about a reality, between informed conformity and changes in habits of mind, between informational learning and transformational learning (Kegan, 2009, p. 42ss).

We could synthesise and illustrate Mezirow's transformative learning process as an ongoing cyclical development:

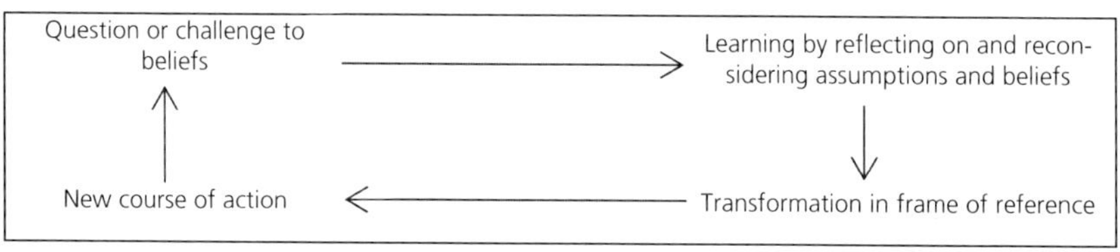

This transformation theory is, in Mezirow's own words, "a constructivist theory of adult learning" (Mezirow, 1991, p. 31).

> Transformative learning is learning that transforms problematic frames of reference (…) to make them more inclusive, discriminating, open, reflective, and emotionally able to change. Such frames of reference (…) are more likely to generate beliefs and opinions that will prove more true or justified to guide action. (Mezirow, 2003, p. 59)

> It holds that beliefs guide action. When the beliefs that guide actions fail or become problematic, our frames of reference may be transformed and learning can occur as individuals critically reflect on their assumptions and beliefs. (Silva, Cahalan & Lacireno-Paquet, 1998, p. 47)

Key concepts of transformative learning:

- Social change: adaptive or transformative?
- Interpretation of experience and of knowledge
- Scheme of reference, meaning, perspective (lens through which one sees his or her reality, the world)
- Emancipation: freedom from previous beliefs and interpretation that distort reality
- Critical reflection of assumptions through which one revises usual ways of seeing oneself and one's relationship, habits of mind or points of view
- Decentration, distanciation, perspective taking
- Banking education (Freire)
- Consciousness raising and change through discourse and dialogue
- Felt (expressed) needs and causes of felt needs
- The mobilising words (Freire)
- Catalyst role of educator

Social and cultural constraints are sources of learning, as they could destabilise one's beliefs, question one's "frame of reference" and destabilise one's "mindsets". Frames of reference are the structures of assumptions through which we understand our experiences. They selectively shape and delimit expectations, perceptions, cognition, and feelings. They set "our line of action" (Mezirow, 1997, p. 5). Frames of reference have two components: habits of mind and points of view (Mezirow, 2000). Habits of mind are broad, habitual ways of thinking (Erickson, 2007, p. 66).

A critical dimension of this learning theory is to consider the reflexive process as a way of becoming independent or autonomous from the context of learning and access higher levels of thinking and to become autonomous from the social context and access higher level of emancipation, thus being able to participate freely in discussions and validate one's personal judgment (Mezirow, 2006). "Through critical reflection, we become emancipated from communication that is distorted by cultural constraints" (Mezirow, 1996, p. 165).

Critical learning is a process that evolves through a number of sequential phases described by Mezirow (1994, p. 224):

1. A disorienting dilemma;
2. Self-examination with feelings of guilt or shame;
3. Critical assessment of assumptions;
4. Recognition that one's discontent and the process of transformation are shared and others have negotiated a similar change;
5. Exploration of options for new roles, relationships, actions;
6. Planning a new course of action;
7. Acquiring knowledge and skills for implementing one's plans;
8. Provisionally trying out new roles;
9. Renegotiating relationships and negotiating new relationships;
10. Building competence and self-confidence in new roles and relationships; and
11. a reintegration into one's life on the basis of conditions dictated by one's new perspective.

Transformative learning aims not only to acquire knowledge through significant experience, but also to acquire a mode to retrieve, test, construct and master new knowledge and new ways to perceive reality. The issue is not only to acquire new knowledge, but to develop new glasses to look differently at reality and existing knowledge. One "reinterprets an old experience (or a new one) from a new set of expectations, thus giving a new meaning and perspective to an old experience" (Mezirow, 1991, p. 11).

Chomsky

There are interesting connections to be drawn between Mezirow's theoretical analysis and the rationalist and semiotic approach of Noam Chomsky (Macedo, 2000). The notions and concepts used by Chomsky converge with Mezirow's vision and expand it beyond structured learning situations to media and work culture. For Chomsky, the individual has a system of common notions that enables him to interpret scattered data. When such data are incoherent with his system of notions, any rational person will favour rigorous analysis and select careful experiment in order to confirm or revise prior conceptions, perceptions, or value orientations. The reflective practice involved in transformative learning is hence more than reflective observation, it is a rational operation involving a search for and an analysis of new information.

Moreover, Chomsky refuses to dissociate educational rights and the right to work freely and intelligently. For him, democracy is a free *and* just society; education cannot be understood outside its relationship with the economy and the issue of work democracy. His semiotic analysis to examine dominant discourse, together with his rational analysis of hidden ideologies is a truly transformative learning exercise. Chomsky looks at the relation between the public and the media or education in the same dialectical and bi-directional ways, i.e. in terms of dominance *and* resistance. Chomsky is in line with James Coleman, one of the main students of education and effects of experience on people's lives, when Coleman concludes from many of his studies that the total effect of home background is considerably greater than the total effect of school variables in determining learner achievement.

Chomsky questions the dominant role of education today. He raises a central question: is the role of education to transmit and accumulate intellectual goods *OR* to create space for inner-driven creativity and the capacity to master information ("providing circumstances in which the normal creative patterns will flourish")? He refers to Dewey's enlarged vision of learning: "The goal of society is not to produce goods, but to produce free human beings associated with one another on terms of equality." For Chomsky, the first mission of education is to develop critical minds.

Mezirow (2003, p. 60) takes a similar view:

> Learning to participate freely and fully in critical-dialectical discourse involves two distinctively adult learning capabilities. One is what Robert Kegan (2000) identified as the development of our uniquely adult capacity to become critically self-reflective. The other is what King and Kitchener (1994) identified as reflective judgment, the capacity to engage in critical-dialectical discourse involving the assessment of assumptions and expectations supporting beliefs, values, and feelings. These adult capabilities are indispensable conditions for fully understanding the meaning of our experience and effective rational adult reasoning in critical discourse and communicative learning.

Exercises and Tasks

Exercise 1

Could you give examples of adaptative and transformative learning experiences?

Exercise 2

What difference do you see between Roger's notion of creativity and the one proposed by Chomsky and Mezirow?

Task 1

According to Mezirow (see text below p. 19), "transformation refers to a movement through time of reformulating reified structures of meaning by reconstructing dominant narratives". Why does Mezirrow insist on the specific condition of adulthood in this context?

Mezirow, J. (2000). Learning to think like an adult: Core concepts of transformation theory. In J. Meziro et. al. (Eds.), *Learning as transformation: Critical perspectives on a theory in progress* (pp. 3-33). San Francisco: Jossey-Bass. http://www.abl-uni-goettingen.de/Material/Mezirow2000.Learning_to_Think_like_an_Adult.pdf

Task 2

In the following short text by Chomsky (1968), he insists on the importance of a rationalist vision of learning. Why, for him, is becoming critically reflective of assumptions so crucial for learning through experience?

Chomsky, Noam (1968). Language and the mind. *Psychology Today*, 48–68.

http://www.stanford.edu/class/symsys100/Chomsky.pdf

Note

See also

Illeris, K. (2003). Learning changes through life. *Lifelong Learning in Europe*, 8, 51-60 http://www.ruc.dk/upload/application/pdf/f665c2a4/Illine.pdf

Illeris, K. (2004). Transformative learning in the perspective of a comprehensive learning theory. *Journal of Transformative Education*, 2, 79-89.

5. Learning Theories: Discussion

As we suggested at the beginning, there are many ways to review the various learning theories. Leonard (2002) organises his review of theories through a classification of four learning paradigms or main learning schools: behaviourism, cognitivism, constructivism, and organisational learning. In his dictionary, he also recalls the major importance of "humanism". Merriam and Caffarella (1999) recognise five major theoretical orientations: behaviourism, cognitivism, humanism, social learning, and constructivism. In Chart 4, we present an expanded and modified synthesis of these classifications, adding two orientations particularly relevant in the specific context of adult learning: the theory of experiential learning and Mezirow's transformation theory.

This classification, as any classification, tends to simplify the complexity of the learning process and to amplify opposition between different theoretical interpretations. A closer look, however, will also reveal some degree of overlap and even convergence between learning theories. Piaget, for example, was influenced by both the behaviourist and Gestalt school of thought when he "proposed that one's internal cognitive structure changes partly as a result of maturational changes in the nervous system and partly as a result of the organism interacting with the environment and being exposed to an increasing number of experiences" (Merriam & Caffarella, 1999, p. 254, 263).

When the constructivist Vygotsky emphasises the importance of confronting people with challenges they can actually master, he is in line with observations made by behaviourists who have shown the value of establishing gradual operational learning objectives, from simple to complex tasks. The concept of "proximal development zone", therefore, could also, to a certain extent, be stated in behaviourist terms.

Similarly, it is true that individuals construct themselves in reflexive interaction with their environment and, to that end, mobilise knowledge and emotional energy. However, this socio-constructivist vision of the learning process should not exclude or play down the constituted procedural and non-procedural knowledge which an individual has to grasp and process mentally in order to better control their life and work context. Through its systematisation of knowledge processing and transmission, the cognitivist approach provides analytical tools for designing learning proposals that build on people's existing tacit and explicit knowledge. In fact, the key notion of lifelong learning has, to a certain extent, been expanded by the cognitivist analysis of the "learning to learn" process.

The humanists and the school of experiential learning have taught us that positive learning experiences help to build learners' self-confidence, enabling them to embrace new situations more creatively. The teacher's role is to facilitate learning as a self-directed process. Such a process can only emerge, according to Rogers, when the proposed learning experience is considered relevant by learners. Not all experiences lead to learning, however. Significant experience is transformed into knowledge when individuals grasp and reflect upon concrete experience and thus become capable of mobilising their new knowledge to operate autonomously in a new context.

Transformation theory, too, borrows many elements from both the socio-constructivist and the humanist theoretical orientations. Learning is not only about acquiring knowledge, but also about mastering the various modes of acquiring, retrieving, testing, constructing, and mobilising new knowledge. Ultimately, it is about developing new ways of perceiving existing knowledge and reality.

Chart 4: Five orientations to learning theories

	Behaviourist	Cognitivist	Cognitivist and social learning	Constructivist and socio-constructivist	Humanist	Experiential learning	Mezirow Chomsky
Learning theorists	Pavlov, Skinner, Thorndike, Watson	Ausubel, Bruner, Gagné, Lewin, Piaget	Bandura	Dewey, Lave, Piaget, Vygotsky	Maslow, Rogers, Knowles	Kolb, Schön	Mezirow Chomsky
View of the learning process	Change in behaviour	Internal mental process (including insight, information process, …)	Interaction with and observation of others in a social context	Construction of meaning from experience	A personal act to fulfill potential	Experience Reflection Experimentation	Distanciation Change through dialogue
Locus of learning	Stimuli in external environment	Internal cognitive structuring	Interaction of person, behaviour, and environment	Internal construction of reality	Affective and cognitive needs	Experience and (tacit and explicit) knowledge	Action and reflection of people upon their world
Purpose of education	Produce behavioural change in desired direction	Develop capacity and skills to learn better	Model new roles and behaviour	Construct knowledge and identity	Become self-actualised, autonomous	Become autonomous Able to adapt to new situation	Transformation of problematic frame of reference
Teacher's role	Arranges environment to elicit desired response	Structures content of learning activity	Models and guides new roles and behaviour	Facilitates and negotiates meaning with learner	Facilitates development of whole person	Facilitates reflective practice on experience	Plays catalyst role
Manifestation in adult learning	Behavioural objectives Competency-based education Skill development and training	Cognitive development Intelligence, learning, and memory as function of age Learning how to learn	Socialisation Social roles Mentoring Locus of control	Self-directed learning Transformation of perspectives Reflexive practice.	Andragogy Self-directed learning Autonomy	Active experimentation Spiral learning Learning as inductive process	Social participation Transformation of perspectives Reflective practice.

Source: Adapted and expanded from Merriam and Cafarella (1999, p. 264).

In other words, even if the analysis in this publication tends to reject narrow behaviourist and cognitivist perspectives in some theoretical frameworks, keeping an informed "agnostic" standpoint on all of them will always remain a creative intellectual attitude for both practitioners and researchers. Furthermore, many theorists, such as Piaget and Bandura, may hardly be confined to any of these categories. Important fundamental contradictions need to be emphasised as well, e.g. between the behaviourists' external approach and the cognitivist school's focus on the internal mental process of learning. Chart 4 tries to synthesise the main characteristics of these various orientations.

The objective of this chapter was to travel across the universe of each of these theories, to look at their analytical tools, and to explore the richness of this scientific heritage as well as its contradictions. The aim was to better equip ourselves intellectually for recognising and understanding the complexity of learning throughout life, a chaotic development or construction which cannot be fully grasped by any single theory.

The questions are numerous. What does it mean to learn? What are the various concepts put forth to understand the complex reality of learning? What are the various possible roles of facilitators in the different learning-teaching contexts? What is the impact of social and cultural environments on learning and learners' aspirations? How important are prior learning experiences? How and under which conditions can individuals construct themselves going through their various life transitions? How can initial education and adult learning contribute to the development of critical minds and creative citizenship?

Moreover, the learning process is complex, not only in terms of its psychological dimension, but also from a social perspective. "The contextual elements represent a critical factor for understanding human learning" (Silberman, 2007, p. 35). The learning experience is also a social process, as we have seen with Bandura (social cognitivism) or with Lave and Wenger (social constructivism). Early on, Dewey insisted that learning is the development of the ability of an individual in society to respond "in an intelligent way" (by inquiring and thinking) to external challenges or difficult contexts.

Learning theories provide schemes of reference for better understanding learning processes, identifying the ways and conditions under which individual adults may develop their capacity for action and expression. However, we also need to understand, from a sociological perspective, the various forms and levels of participation in adult learning activities and the factors predicting the different profiles of participation observed across societies.

Part Two:
Theories of Adult Learning and Education Participation

6. Introduction to Theories of Adult Learning and Education Participation

Adult learning and education is a rapidly expanding domain, but a difficult one to map because of the dispersed reality of organised learning, the diversity of provision, and the complexity of monitoring formal and non-formal learning activities. Institutional statistics are relevant when education providers are institutionalised within a common framework, e.g. at the initial primary, secondary, and post-secondary levels. However, this is not the same in adult learning, with its vast diversity of providers, interventions, and supported self-learning initiatives. Only by doing household surveys could we arrive at a full picture of adult population participation in organised learning activities. The first such survey was administered in the United States in 1965 (Johnstone & Rivera, 1965). Since then, such surveys have become the normal procedure to monitor the situation and evaluate the impact of adult learning policies in advanced industrialised countries (Eurostats 2009; OECD, 2005; TNS Infratest, 2007; Aldridge & Tuckett, 2007; Peters, 2004; Cross, 1982; Rubenson, 1977). The first international comparative analysis based on such statistical data appeared in 1997 (Bélanger & Valdivielso, 1997; Bélanger & Tuijnman, 1997).

Of course, monitoring organised education and training activities through participation surveys can merely provide us with a limited portrait of the full reality of adult learning, showing us only the visible part of the learning iceberg (Livingston, 2003). We should not reduce our vision of adult learning and education participation to structured learning activities just because informal learning is difficult to document, however. Studies monitoring informal adult learning either statistically (Livingston, 2003, 2001; Statistics Canada, 2003) or qualitatively through biographical research (Alheit, Bron-Wojciechowska, Brugger & Dominicé, 1995) or through recognition of experiential learning (Colardyn & Bjornavold, 2004; Evans, 2000) show the importance of tacit learning and the informal development of skills and knowledge.

The question we will address in Part 2 of this study guide is not only **who** tends to participate (or doesn't) in **what kind of activities**, but also **why** different groups of adults tend to participate (or don't) and **what these differences in participation mean** in people's learning biographies. A variety of theories have been developed in response to these questions.

7. An Empirical Portrait of Adult Participation in Organised Adult Learning and Education (ALE) Activities

7.1 The unequal development of adult learning participation

Who participates in what kinds of activities? To answer this question in an internationally comparable perspective, given the lack of international harmonisation in most surveys, we will have to rely on data extracted from the 1994-1998 **International Adult Literacy Survey** (IALS) administered in 18 countries by OECD (in cooperation with ETS and Statistics Canada) through a representative sample of the adult population in each society. The IALS questionnaire contained a set of questions on adult learning and education participation, allowing researchers to build a comparable dependant variable (i.e. participation in organised learning activities during the 12 months preceding the interview). Unfortunately, the IALS survey only covered the adult population aged 16 to 65. Consequently, the participation of senior citizens could not be addressed from a comparative standpoint, the obvious high relevance of the age variable in lifelong learning research notwithstanding. We will therefore have to refer to specific non-comparable surveys to study participation patterns after retirement age.

We will rely on the statistical analysis of the IALS 2003 survey done by Desjardins, Rubenson and Milana and published by UNESCO-IIEP in 2006. The German data introduced in some tables come from a survey carried out annually by the German Infratest Research Centre (TNS Infratest, 2008). The reader should be aware that data between Germany and the other countries may not be compared directly. We introduce these data despite their limitations, however, remaining aware of a margin of discrepancy for inter-country comparability that could easily exceed 10%. We will also use the **Adult education survey** administered by Eurostat within their "Population and Social Conditions" section.[2]

Today, participation in organised adult learning activities is a common feature in each and all advanced industrial countries. Table 1, based on recent

2 Eurostats http://epp.eurostat.ec.europa.eu/cache/ITY_OFFPUB/KS-SF-09-044/EN/KS-SF-09-044-EN.PDF. See also Eurostat's Continuing Training Survey (CVTS).

data (2007), shows the participation rate in the overall domain of adult learning and education (ALE) in seven European countries, ranging from more than 70% in Sweden to 20% in Portugal. It is interesting to notice that, when the ALE participation rate in a country exceeds 40%, the total number of participating adults tends to prevail over the overall number of young people enrolled in formal initial education. And, as in the case of the Nordic countries, when the ALE participation rate exceeds 55%, the total volume of organised adult learning activities tends to even exceed the overall volume of formal initial education at the primary, secondary, and post-secondary levels combined. Adult education participation is no more a marginal reality. The increasing economic, social, and cultural need for individuals capable of acting and expressing themselves more autonomously for an increased and more autonomous capacity of action and expression has transformed the learning demands of men and women.

Table 1: General ALE Participation Rate (2007)

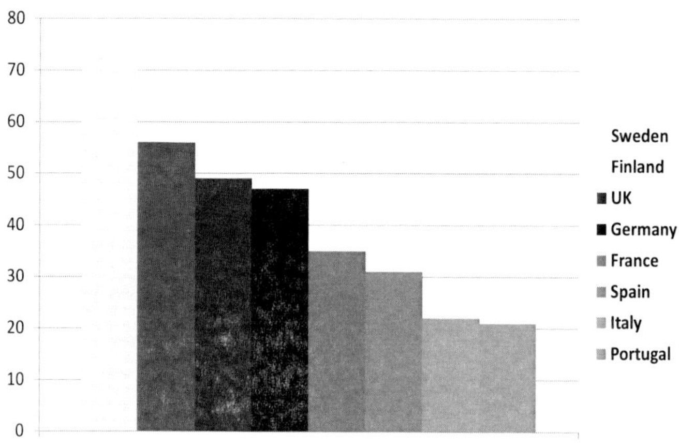

Source: Eurostats (Boateng, 2009)

National education scenes, in other words, are undergoing sweeping change, a phenomenon still poorly recognised. This shifting balance between initial and adult education is the result of an overall and steady growth of adult participation in learning activities since the 1970s, a trend that may be observed in all countries. Table 2, referring to the German context, offers a typical example of this common movement. Other examples could be observed in Canada and the US between 1994 and 2003 (+14%) and in Norway (+6.3%) between 1998 and 2003 (IALS 1994-1998 and ALLS 2003 surveys). Four factors, all in continuous expansion, are at work driving this development: rising average level of initial education among the adult population, the ongoing introduction of new information technology both at work and in daily life, a higher proportion of out-of-work periods along the adult life path, and the multiplication of work and non-work transitions throughout one's life course.

Table 2: General ALE Participation Rate in Germany 1987-2007 (%)

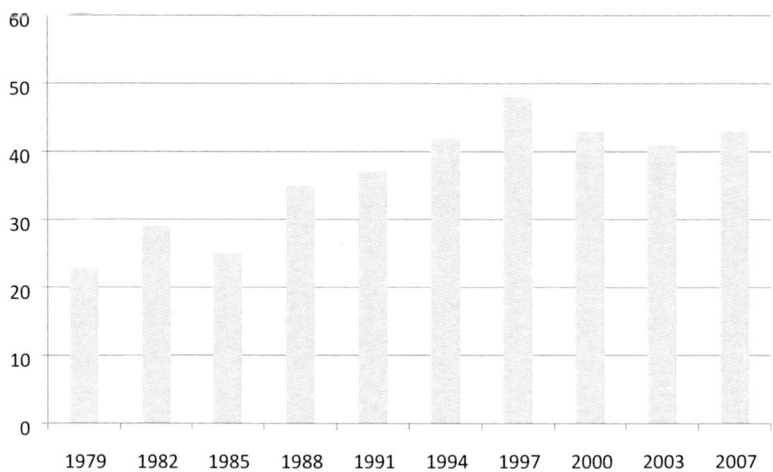

Source: Infratest (von Rosenbladt et al. 2008)

Beyond this common trend, two important disparities need to be underlined (see Table 1 for 2007 and Table 3 for 1998). First, the development of adult education is uneven between industrialised countries. As we could see in Tables 1 and 3, participation rates differ significantly between countries (from 70 to 20%). Second, the balance between work-related and non-work-related adult learning events varies considerably. In the Northern European countries (see Table 3), we observe roughly the same level of activity in both areas, whereas in Australia, Canada, Czech Republic, and Hungary, the rate of participation in non-job related adult learning and education is up to three times lower than in work-related activities.

Table 3: General ALE Participation Rate (1994-1998)

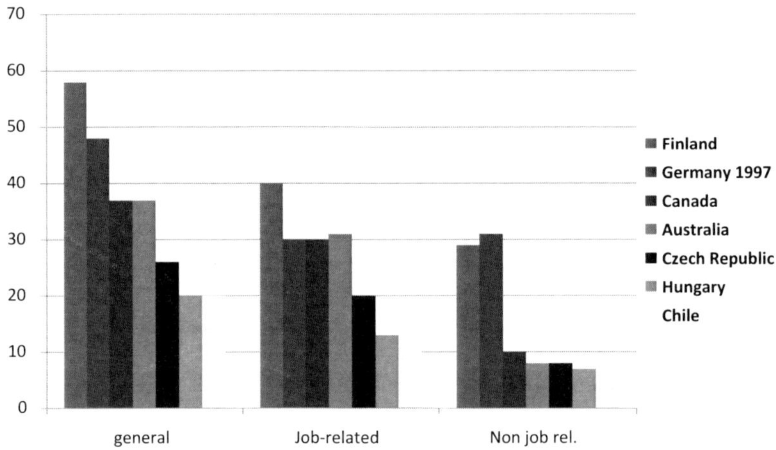

Source: IIEP 2006; Germany Infratest (von Rosenbladt & Bilger, 2008)

It is also important to note that, if ALE participation rates tend to increase over time, this trend is not always continuous. We observe some periods of decrease as well, e.g. in Italy between 1998 and 2003 (-3.6%), in the United Kingdom between 2006 and 2008, involving a loss of 1.5 million participants (*Times Educational Supplement*, 2008, May 16, p. 7), and in Germany between 1997 and 2007, when ALE participation decreased by 5% and even 8% within the active population, especially in industrial sectors (TNS Infratest, 2008).

7.2 The social profile of participants in adult education and learning activities

A cross-country analysis of variations in ALE participation rates regarding demographic, socio-economic, contextual, and cultural variables yields specific profiles of adult education participants. The strongest trend to be observed in all countries, albeit at different levels, is the correlation between initial education and ALE participation illustrated in Table 4. In all countries, the likelihood of ALE participation tends to be three or even more times higher for those with advanced levels of prior formal schooling. Learning life courses tend to be cumulative. The more you have, the more you will get. Of course, social reproduction is never absolute. The percentage (observed between 1994 and 1998) of "non-typical" participants is much lower in the US than it is in Finland and the UK. In these latter two countries, one adult out of three escaped statistical probability and participated in learning activities. These data indicate that policies, practices, and cultural contexts do make a difference.

Table 4: Initial Education and ALE Participation Rate (1994-1998)

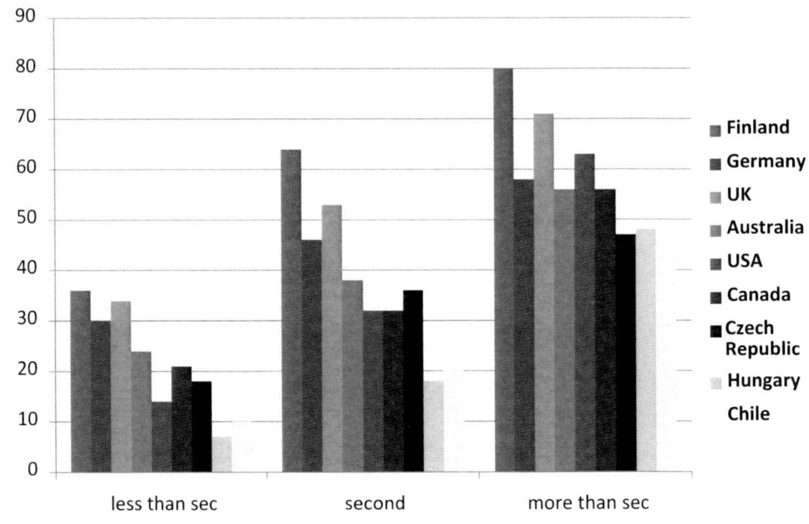

Source: IIEP 2006

The impact of formal education is not only intra-generational. As we can see in Table 5, the ALE participation of the next generation is significantly associated with parents' level of initial education.

Table 5: Parents Education and ALE Participation Rate

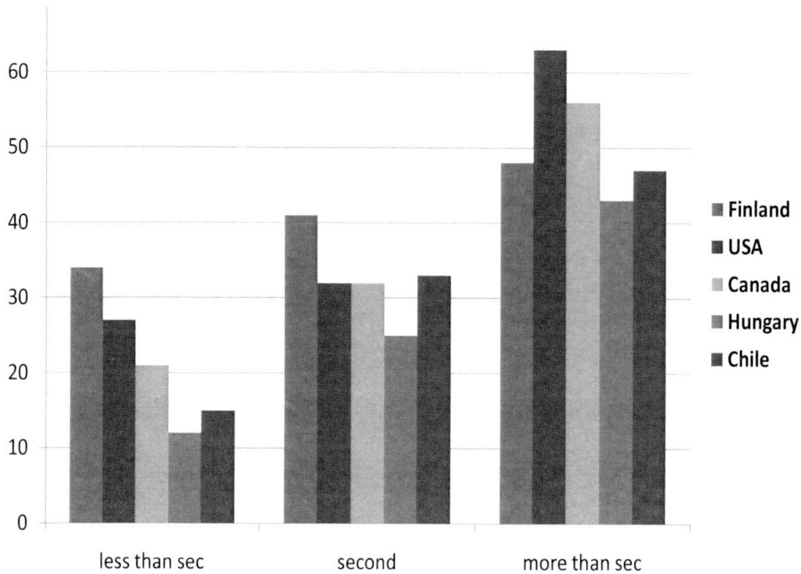

Source: IIEP 2006

Furthermore, the level of occupational qualification is associated with adult education participation (see Table 6). Low-qualified blue collar workers tend to be two to three times less likely to participate in ALE than highly qualified white collar workers. Data collected between 1994 and 1998 (Table 6) show greater discrepancies in this regard than more recent data from 2007 (Table 7), indicating some improvement. This trend, suggesting a positive link between ALE participation and the level of formal qualification, is especially relevant not only in terms of social reproduction, but also in the current context of industrial transformation. New knowledge and skills requirements are being created at all occupational levels by the ongoing introduction of new information technology and new modes of production related to new quality control systems and the diversification of production. Its impact is felt across the occupational pyramid. These changes, pressed on by global competition, are transforming skills requirements and hence the learning demand at all levels of qualification. Again, however, responses to these changes in 1994-1998 and even in 2007 vary considerably across countries.

Table 6: Occupation and ALE Participation Rate

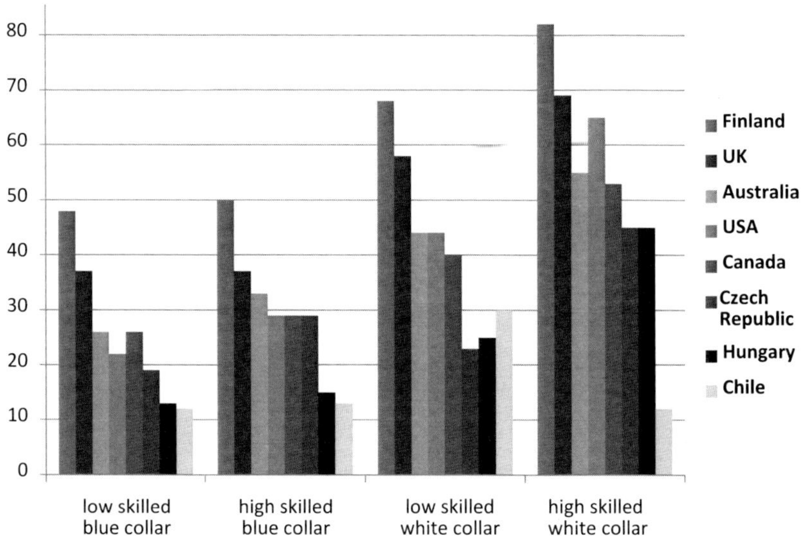

Source: IIEP 2006

Table 7: Occupation and ALE Participation Rate (2007)

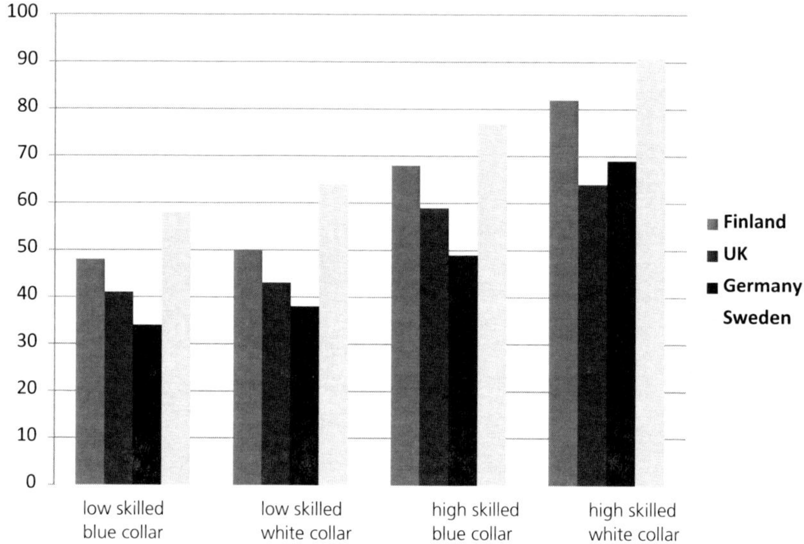

Source: Eurostats, Boatang, 2008

The correlation between ALE participation and gender is more complex (see Table 8). In 1994-1998, male participation rates tend to exceed female rates by a small margin, with the exception of Finland, where women participate at significantly higher levels than men. In 2007, we may observe varying gender differences in a number of European countries (Boatang, 2008). Countries with high participation rates have a higher proportion of participating females. In Germany, France, and Austria, in contrast, male participation rates are higher than those of females.

Table 8: Gender and ALE Participation Rate (1994-1998)

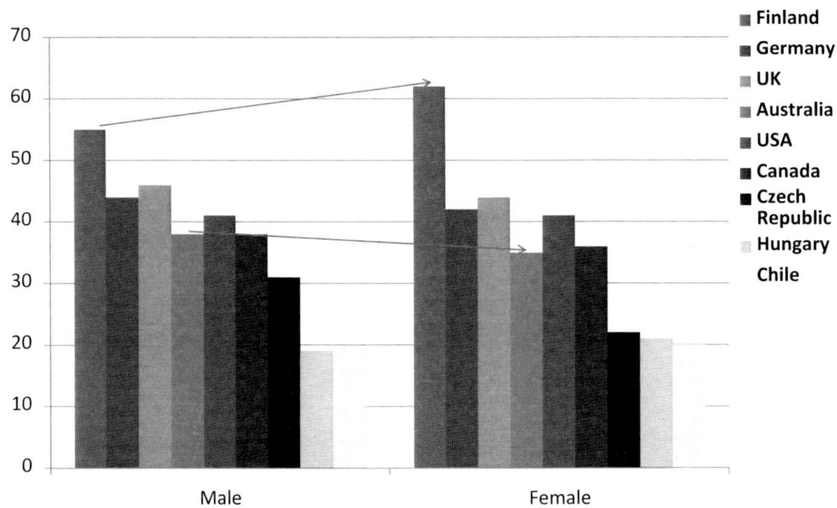

Source: IIEP 2006

Data from Table 9 clearly shows that lifelong learning is not yet a lifelong phenomenon among persons aged 55 and older. Participation rates, which start to decline as soon as people turn 45, drop even further in the age group of 55-64 years. The 2007 Eurostats survey (Boateng, 2008) indicates that countries with high rates of participation now show a much higher proportion of 55- to 64-year-olds participating in adult education and training. Sweden stands out considerably from the other countries with a participation rate of 60.7% for this age group, followed by Norway (41.2%), Finland (37.8%), United Kingdom (37.0%), and Germany (28.2%).

We observe a further decrease in ALE participation among 64-plus-year-olds, precisely at a time when people, paradoxically, have more free time. In the UK, for example, decline in adult education participation is particularly abrupt among 55-plus-year-olds. Only 31 per cent of adults aged 55-64, 21 per cent aged 65-74, and 15 per cent of those aged 75 and over view themselves as learners (Aldridge & Tuckett, 2007). In the UK, less than 10% of the population aged 65 and over report their involvement in current learning events.

Table 9: Age and ALE Participation Rate (1994-1998)

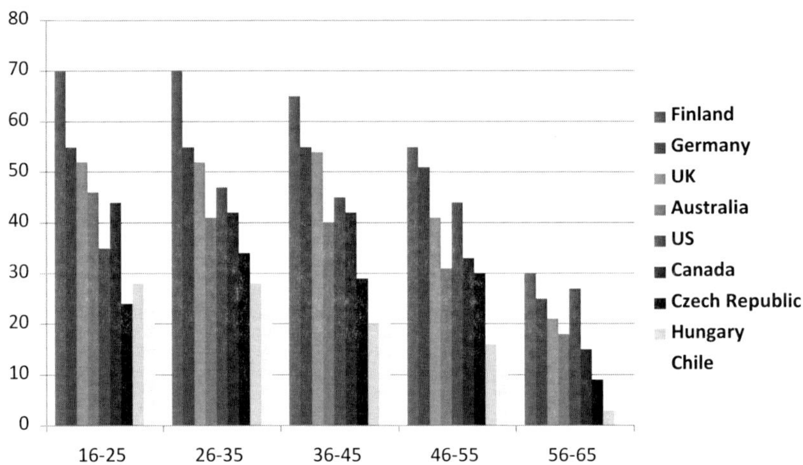

Source: IIEP 2006

Employment status is another decisive factor for ALE participation. In 1994-1998 (Table 10) and in 2007 (Boateng, 2008), unemployed and inactive people account for the largest proportion of non-participants in all countries.

Table 10: Employment Status and ALE Participation Rate

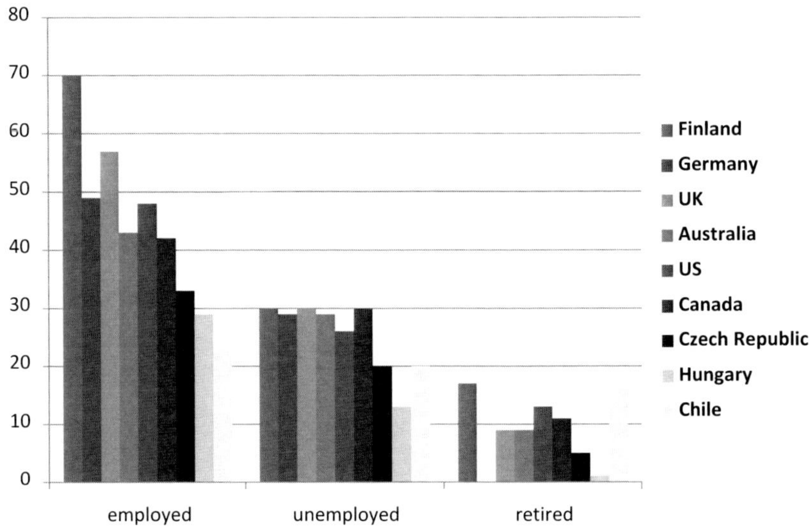

Source: IIEP 2006

Rural and urban statuses have different effects in each country (Aldridge & Tuckett 2007). The rural population tends to participate more in Finland and the U.S., but significantly less in Australia, Canada, Czech Republic, Hungary, and Chile.

Table 11: Rural-Urban Status and ALE Participation

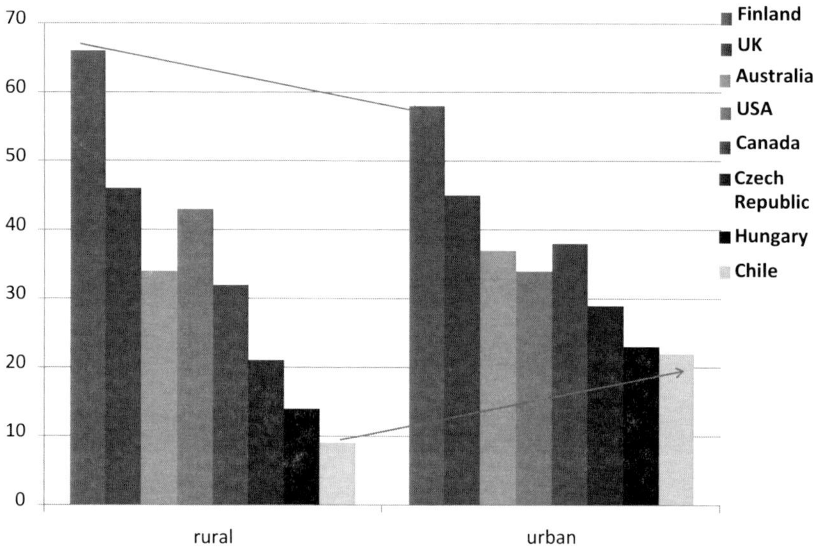

Source: IIEP 2006

Work context is another important factor influencing ALE participation. Firm size provides a case in point, for example. In all countries (see Table 12), the rate of participation in structured adult learning activities tends to increase with the number of an organisation's employees.

Table 12: Size of Firma- and Job-related ALE

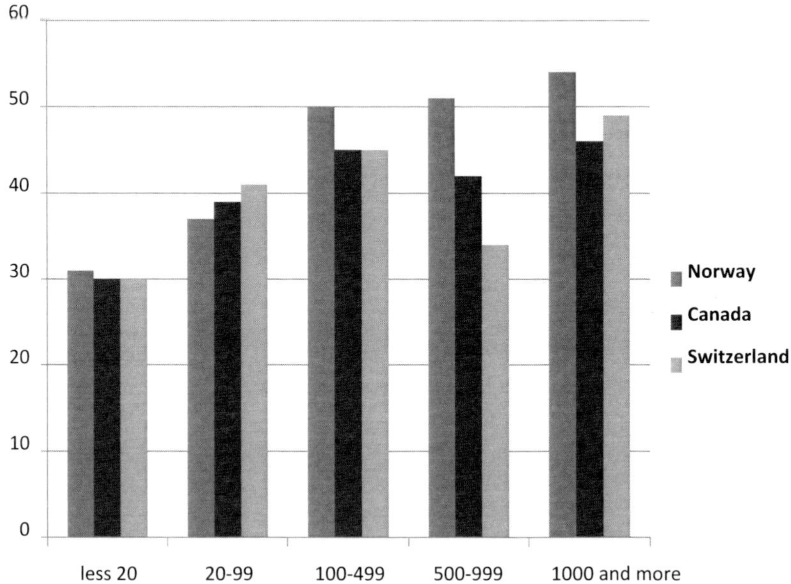

Source: IIEP 2006

Likewise, the extent to which employees have to use written communication on a daily basis impacts the level of ALE participation. We can expect (see Table 13) higher rates of participation in learning activities in firms that feature a lot of reading- and writing-intensive positions.

Table 13: Reading Practice in Firms and ALE Participation

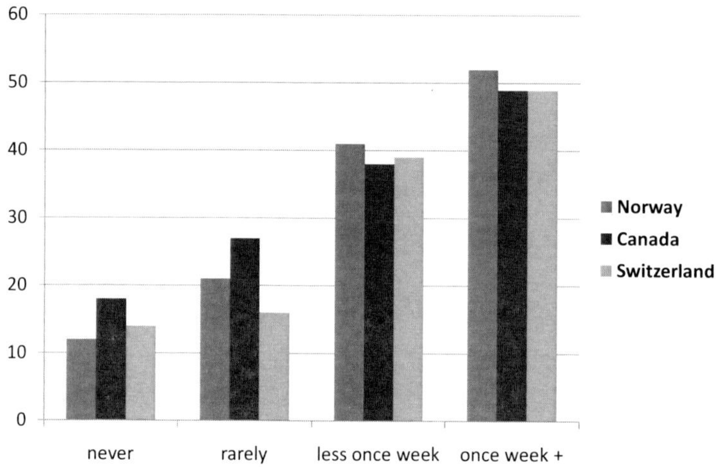

Source: IIEP 2006

It is also of much interest to revisit these different factors according to various types of adult learning and education. Table 14 shows the impact of employment status, age, gender, and citizenship on the rate of participation in work and non-work related adult learning and education. The data are from the 2007 German survey (TNS Infratest, 2008).

Table 14: Participation Patterns and Orientation of ALE

Variables	Work-oriented	Non-work-oriented	Total participation
Active population	34	29	49
Non active population	8	24	29
19-24	22	35	47
25-34	31	27	46
35-44	32	29	47
45-64	22	25	38
Male	29	26	44
Female	24	29	42
Born in Germany	28	28	44
Migrants	18	28	39

Source: Infratest 2008

Unsurprisingly, work and non-work related participation rates vary in relation to people's participation or non-participation in the formal economy. However, it is interesting to discover how these two types of learning also seem to vary according to other variables. While young adults give priority to work-related adult learning, senior workers tend to participate more in non-work related activities, albeit not exclusively. The same is true in terms of gender, with slightly more women giving preference to non-work related learning than males. The migrant population shows much stronger participation in non-work-related activities than in work-related ones, most probably due to their high levels of enrollment in second language education courses.

Finally, what may be concluded from this overview of participation statistics? First, people's probability to participate in various kinds of adult learning and education activities varies across countries, which implies that national contexts, and national policy contexts in particular, can indeed make a difference, as may be seen when comparing countries in Northern Europe, North America, Southern as well as Eastern Europe. The proactive policies implemented in Northern European countries, for example, have led to higher levels of ALE participation among less formally educated adults and less qualified workers (Rubenson, 2003).

Second, empirical data show that participation in adult learning activities varies considerably according to demographic, socio-economic, and cultural factors. Consider, for example, the impact of initial education or the decreasing level of participation according to age cohort.

Third, these factors mutually reinforce each other, adding up their respective impact in positive and negative ways. Factor analysis helps us to see such revealing configurations of variables, for example, when comparing employment status, age, and initial education.

Table 15: Combined Factors and ALE Participation (1994-1998)

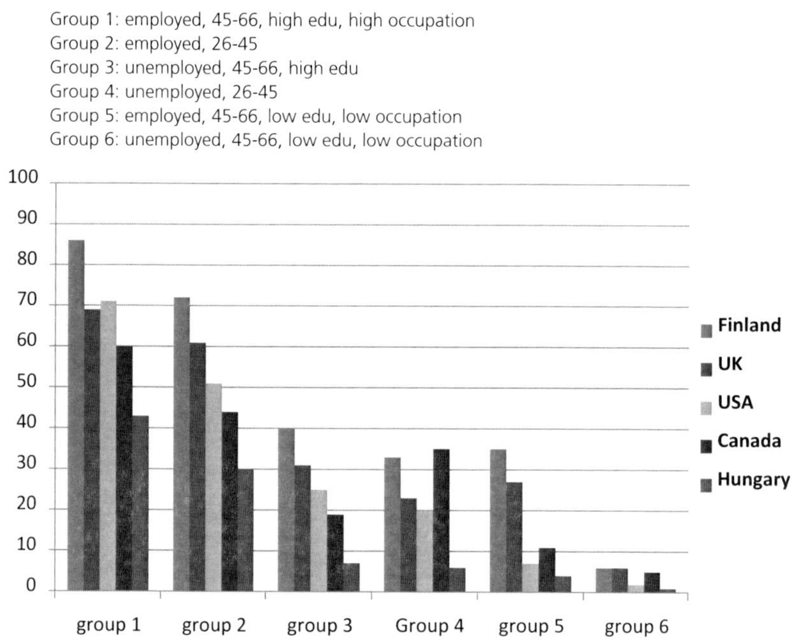

Source: IIEP 2006

Table 15 clearly illustrates these extreme variations in ALE participation according to six configurations combining these factors. If you are employed, have a high level of initial education, and hold a high-status job, you are six to ten times more likely to participate in adult learning than if you are unemployed, completed only basic schooling, and have less qualification. If you are young, your employment status will probably be the main determining factor. If you are currently unemployed, but hold advanced educational credentials, you are more likely to participate in ALE programs, except in Canada, where intensive programs for unemployed persons may make a difference.

Exercises and Tasks

Exercise 1

If you look at your parents and their level of participation or non-participation in adult learning, which of the factors outlined above do you think have influenced their decision to participate or not?

Exercise 2

What significant differences do you see in the participation of the active and of the non-active population? Is the situation the same in other countries that you happen to know?

Exercise 3

What links do you see between the data presented in Table 5 and Table 4, i.e. between the influence of parents' education and the influence of participants' initial education?

Task 1

In this classic text by Cookson (1986), the various factors impinging on adult education participation are presented and discussed as a complex chain of conditions perceived by individuals. Do such factors have the same influence and interconnection in work-oriented learning as in general adult education?

Cookson, Peter S. (1986). A framework for theory and research on adult education participation. *Adult Education Quarterly*, 36, 130-141.
http://aeq.sagepub.com/content/36/3/130.full.pdf+html

Task 2

One of the mishaps of adult education participation studies is the under-representation of informal learning. Livingstone (2002) wrote about the invisible part of the iceberg and the underemployment of the existing pool of knowledge and skills informally acquired. Could you give examples of such bias in public representation of the ALE domain and of the consequences in the development of learning societies?

Livingstone, David 2002). Mapping the iceberg. *NALL Working Paper* 54.

http://www.nall.ca/res/54DavidLivingstone.pdf

8. Analysis of ALE Participation

8.1. Theoretical analysis

We have seen that ALE participation is shaped by numerous factors: cultural predisposition, socio-economic status, living conditions, public policy, work environment, and institutional provision of learning opportunities. Once such factors have been identified, the challenge is to analyze their interrelations in order to understand the processes and mechanisms of such participation.

Various attempts have been made to go beyond demographic and social mapping of adult learning participation (Courtney, 1992; Wikelund, Reder & Hart-Landsberg, 1992) in order to understand the social dynamics at work.

Early on, a structural analytical approach was developed in France, which has since been expanded. Drawing on Bourdieu's sociological analysis (Bourdieu & Passeron, 1970) researchers sought to explain ALE participation patterns by looking at an individual's position in society and at their workplace as well as by studying structural inequalities in the distribution of learning opportunities. Such studies (De Montlibert, 1973, 1977) tend to insist that adult education is largely governed by the logic of social reproduction. According to this point of view, adult learners' social origin, their parents' educational status (see Table 5 above), and their family's cultural influence and social position (Gorard, Renold & Fevre, 1998) all serve to determine the level and kind of their ALE participation. De Montlibert shows, for example, that adults participating in ALE tend to be individuals who, in terms of their social background, should have succeeded earlier at school, using adult education to later regain their socially expected socio-economic position. In other words, participation is influenced by the unequal distribution of cultural capital. Who has more gets more.

However, the reproduction of structured inequality is relative. Table 5, for example, shows that a significant percentage of adults with low-education parents do participate in adult learning activities in spite of their social origin. This is especially true for Finland. We also observe (see Table 4) a participation rate of 30% and more among adults holding less than a secondary school diploma in Finland, Germany, and the United Kingdom. Similarly (see Table 6), 48% and 58% of low-skilled blue collar workers in Finland and Sweden respectively participated in organised learning activities in 2007. Despite a significant tendency towards the social reproduction of inequality in adult education participation patterns, therefore, we need to explain why significant groups of adults do participate in ALE, after all, defying such theoretical predictions. Furthermore, if social reproduction turns out to be relative, what are the factors that help explain both prevalent trends and significant atypical patterns?

Psycho-social approaches have been developed to explain these participation patterns by looking at various motivational factors driving an individual's decision to participate or not, e.g. occupational projects and social expectation (Blair, McPake & Munn, 1995). They distinguish between extrinsic and intrinsic motives, between exchange value and content or process-oriented objectives. As early as in 1961, Cyril Houle (1961) developed a typology of people's motivations as a key factor in their decision to participate in ALE.

The most important psycho-social model for explaining ALE participation patterns was conceived by Cross (1982) and further developed by other researchers trying to understand the barriers that different social groups tend to face (Rubenson & Xu, 1997; Cookson, 1986; Henry & Basile, 1994; Scanlan & Darkenwald, 1984; Darkenwald & Valentine, 1985; Silva, Cahalan & Lacireno-Paquet, 1998). Cross developed a composite model that frames adult participation as a result of a complex chain of responses to conditions perceived by individuals. Cross distinguishes three series of factors or barriers to participation: institutional, situational, and dispositional barriers.

Institutional barriers include procedures and types of education provision preventing or discouraging participation, e.g. courses not offered, distance, inconvenient timing and scheduling, lack of formal qualifications required by an institution, mismatch between demand and responses, lack of flexibility of provision, lack of information and of guidance services.

Situational barriers are obstacles arising from one's economic and social situation at a given time. Often expressed as "lack of time!" and "no money!", such barriers are linked to different life and work situations and conditions such as low initial education, socio-economic status, age, parental and family roles (reconciliation of roles), employment situation, work context (economic sector, firm size, regular use of written information), or lack of public or private financial support. Within situational barriers, as shown by most surveys, the level of initial education is the most important predictor of participation in adult learning.

Dispositional barriers refer to people's attitudes and perceptions of themselves as learners, e.g. low readiness to learn, sense of learning inefficiency, low self-confidence or self-esteem, lack of work or and work related personal objectives or projects, sense of irrelevance and uselessness of learning, weakly felt needs, language barriers, perceived health condition, socio-cultural practices (reading habits, social participation).

Among the dispositional barriers to ALE participation, Darkenwald and Valentine (1985) draw an important distinction between psycho-social obstacles (perception of education or of oneself as a learner) and informational obstacles (lack of awareness of learning opportunities). They go on to highlight six important factors that tend to keep people from engaging in structured adult learning: lack of confidence, lack of course relevance, time constraints, low personal priority, cost, and personal or family problems.

Across the participation literature, the single most crucial predictor of participation in adult learning activities is a person's level of initial education. People's initial schooling experience and their cultural relationship with formal education tend to structure their representations and attitudes toward learning and education. Longer initial education, positive previous learning experiences, and hence stronger education expectancy help explain the differences in people's likelihood to participate in adult learning and education and, to a certain degree, the small but significant differences between male and female participation. Prior education also influences an individual's ability to express unmet learning demands and aspirations (Doray, Bélanger & Labonté, 2005; Doray & Livingstone, 2002). The impact of cultural capital is even broader, however. Whether someone likes to read and write tends to influence their level of participation. People who read and write a lot, for example, are much more likely to participate in adult learning and education than people who spend a lot of time watching TV.

In the wake of the pioneering work of De Sanctis (1988), some researchers focused their research on the **non-public** aspects of adult education (Hédoux, 1982; Quigley & Arrowsmith, 1997; Reay, Ball & David, 2002), the **a-typical** participant (Bélanger, Doray, Labonté & Levesque, 2005), or the **non-traditional** participant (Bowl, 2001) in order to understand the factors that could explain such "unusual" types of participation. Weak motivation, for example, may be overcome by positive community support or by the education provider's strong institutional reputation (Henry & Basile, 1994). Special policies geared towards single-parent families can help reverse socially predictable trends (Doray, Bélanger, Motte & Labonté, 2005). Based on such findings, researchers are in a position to propose policy shifts in order to alter the conditions that tend to shape ALE participation patterns.

Life conditions, both at home and at the workplace, tend to determine people's access to two key resources: time and money which, in turn, may have a negative impact on adult learning participation. Financial factors include direct costs and less visible indirect charges. Working conditions also influence participation through the unequal allocation of learning resources and opportunities within and between firms (Gagnon, 2004; Gagnon, Doray & Bélanger, 2004).

In most surveys, when people are asked about their reasons for non-participation, they most often mention a **lack of time**. The response pattern does not vary significantly across countries (see Table 16). We will need to look at the specific factors behind this overt and general reason, however. As illustrated in Table 16, the most frequently expressed reason for non-participation is a gendered one because of gender differences in the work-family-education equilibrium and in the prevailing division of domestic labours.

Table 16: Main reasons expressed for non participation

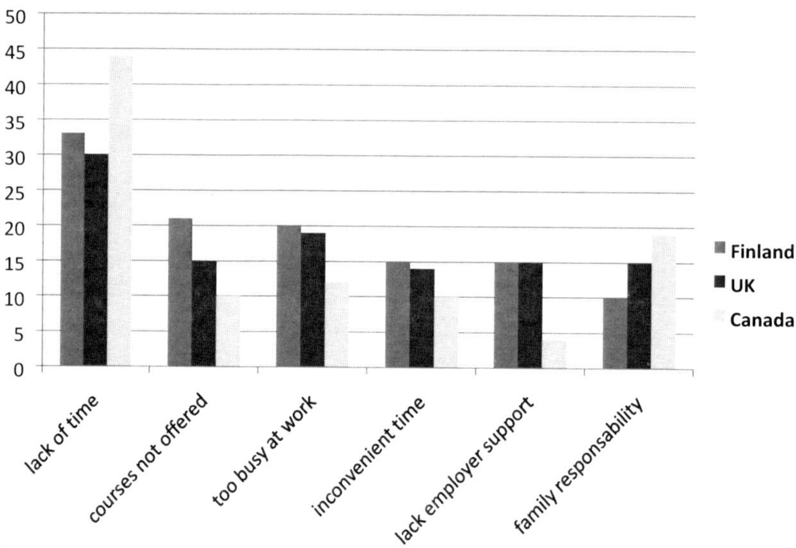

Source: IIEP 2006, Data 1994-1998

In *The Future of Lifelong Learning* (Schuller & Watson, 2009), a recent report by the National Institute of Adult Continuing Education (NIACE), a non-governmental organisation for adult learning in England and Wales, the time factor is interpreted in the perspective of changing life courses and biographical patterns. It is precisely during the "rush hour" life phase, i.e. between the age of 25 and 50, that people tend to mention this reason most frequently. This period is indeed often characterised by intensive work-related learning demands on individuals and by demanding parental responsibility.

Explaining participation patterns through biographical analysis helps to shed new light on the modulation of lifelong learning across adult life courses.

Many issues remain to be addressed, however, and should be part of the future research agenda:

- the absence of recent internationally comparable data,
- the relations between informal learning and participation in structured learning,
- the lifelong continuity of participation or non-participation as a result of various factors cumulating over time,
- empirical tests of the various theoretical models using internationally comparable data,
- the undocumented reality of a multiplicity of learning motives involved in people's decisions to participate in ALE,
- a better understanding of the relationship between work and non-work related adult learning,
- the invisible reality of informal learning.

In order to be able to analyze the situation across time and national contexts, the most important issue for all countries is conducting regular and comparative household surveys to monitor the diverse and dispersed field of adult learning and education, the way it is done in Germany and the UK on a regular basis. Without having such a basic information base, theories will remain untested and, more importantly, participation studies will not be able to contribute fully to information-based policy development.

Exercises and Tasks

Exercise 1

Could you give other examples of different combinations of factors (age, work environment, policies of providers, cultural milieu, workplace, guidance and information services, etc) that could help overturn prevailing trends?

Exercise 2

How do you explain differences in male and female patterns of participation in work and non-work related adult learning?

Exercise 3

Referring to Cross' three sets of factors, why do you think men tend to participate less in non-work related adult learning?

Task

In their "inquiry into the future of lifelong learning" in the UK, Schuller and Watson (2009) propose to base lifelong learning policy on a new model of the educational life course, with four key stages (up to 25, 25-50, 50-75, 75+). Looking at ALE participation patterns in your country, would you propose similar or different key stages? Why?

Schuller, T. & Watson, D. (2009). *Learning through life: Inquiry into the future for lifelong learning. Summary.* National Institute of Adult Continuing Education.

http://www.niace.org.uk/lifelonglearninginquiry/docs/IFLL-summary-english.pdf

8.2 Biographical analysis of adult education participation

Transitions, either professional or personal, are heuristic moments enabling researchers to capture the meaning of people's various recourses to active learning practices in late modernity. Some transitions are institutionalised, of course, such as children attending primary and secondary education. However, such foreseeable and even mandatory life transitions do not characterise people's biographies in late modernity any more.

Biographies are becoming a succession of life transitions of various types, including occupational mobility, migration, health-related incidents, and intimate shifts in private life. Far from being exceptional, transitions have emerged as an important constituent of contemporary life. Professional mobility, job insecurity, periods of illness, changes in people's private lives, the successive transformation of parental roles, discontinuities in the passage from adolescence to adulthood, and the desynchronisation of people's retirement age are all parts of life courses today. Transitions may also be voluntary, prompted by individuals themselves and, in certain cases, prepared long in advance, such as a professional promotion or a change in private life. However, certain transitions may also be enforced or prompted by a third party, or they may be accidental, e.g. in the case of illness.

Biographical transitions could influence adult participation in learning and education in several ways. A professional mobility project may motivate individuals to take part in education and training programs, for example. Transitions in other life contexts may affect the availability of learning resources either by introducing people in new networks or by consequent gain or loss of social capital. Reciprocally, transitions may be influenced by people's representations of education or by the value they attach to it and their expectancy to participate successfully in learning activities. Their ability and propensity to mobilise learning resources may be significantly altered in this case. The availability of educational opportunities and the way they are organised may also structure participation.

Furthermore, life transitions are either lived as an other-directed and passive process or as an inner-directed and active one. Some people experience these transitions powerlessly, going through them in a passive and dependent mode. Others, confronted with similar discontinuities in their life-course, will tend to use life transitions as an opportunity for developing new capacities for action to help them pilot this uncertain phase in their biography. For these people, each learning episode undertaken becomes a special moment requiring them to acquire new rules and roles (Tinto, 1993) and, as a consequence, to mobilise their knowledge and savoir-faire (Lave & Wenger, 1991). Even back in 1982, Cross identified transitions in people's life courses as potential momentum or phases of intensive learning. People seeking to actively pilot their transitions also tend to participate actively in either formal or informal learning activities.

The gradual deinstitutionalisation of life courses therefore requires people to gain new skills for navigating their lives. It involves "a redeployment of learning opportunities in individual and social spaces which characterises adult life today" (Dominice, 1999, p. 143). It requires **biographicity**, i.e. an "individual knowledge resource to deal with modern reality" (Alheit & Dausien, 2000), a qualification for which no curriculum exists. In a society of incertitude (Beck, 1992; Beck & Beck-Gernsheim, 2002), reflexive modernity compels individuals to adopt biographical construction, to develop coherence, and to give meaning to their lives. Living one's life has become unpredictable.

In biographical analysis, the analytical perspective is twofold. First, it focuses on people's quest for biographical coherence, on their construction of identity, their attempt to reduce biographical inconsistency and pilot their life course. The second focus is on spaces at meso levels for supporting individuals' ongoing construction of their biography and for actualising the "potential of life not yet lived". "The learning processes", writes Alheit (1994), "between structure and subjectivity are manifold, but they can only be understood if we do justice to *both* poles: the structural framework of conditions governing our lives and the spontaneous dispositions that we adopt towards ourselves".

A more macro-social biographical approach seeks to identify the meanings that people give to their learning life course or their "learning career". It does so by conducting cross-generational interviews (Antikainen & Juha, 2002) or by studying individuals and organising focus groups of participants and non-participants (Crossan, Field, Gallacher & Merrill, 2003). People's visions of learning and education do in fact differ across generations and various economic situations and contexts. Whereas completing initial education was the ultimate goal for the older generation, it is now taken for granted by the younger generation (Antikainen, 2002). Similarly, adult learning is no longer an exceptional event in one's adult life. Moreover, classical socio-economic variables cannot fully explain ALE participation patterns, particularly regarding the significant and growing number of atypical cases. Gallacher and his colleagues discovered that critical events in individual biographies have an autonomous influence beyond classical socio-demographic factors and could thus help to explain "unusual" cases. "Critical incidents such as divorce, bereavement or redundancy can act as turning points which lead people to reappraise their lives, and consider the need for some form of change" (Gallacher, Field, Merrill & Crossan, 2002).

Participation theories could borrow elements from both approaches by studying the connections between transitions and participation, putting special emphasis on individuals' various social experiences or their quest for more biographical autonomy. In such a theoretical context, transitions are regarded as identifiable moments and objective life events. In this respect, learning events that look similar in terms of statistics could have very different meanings. Biographical research contributes to our ability to grasp the meanings that people give to their life and learning events and to recognise the cultural orientation these events carry for the subject.

Transitions or life crossroads may offer an opportunity for rupture in one's educational biography, for overcoming one's prior perceptions of education and one's own capacities. Yet such rupture, as we have observed among participants, requires a certain degree of affirmative action, special peer support, and a new learning environment. In people's strategy to cope with the risks associated with any major life shift, the active learning component in such transitions tends to be critically important. As people try to proactively manage their life course when arriving at such a crossroads, their biographicity may thus be enhanced. That's why the socially constructed nature of both adult learning provision and expression of learning demand could alter people's biographicity by creating inequitable possibilities to succeed in such a transition.

Actively navigating one's biography is closely associated with the general economy of lifelong learning which, in today's societies, tends to distribute learning resources and opportunities, throughout people's life course, in unequal ways.

Exercises and Tasks

Exercise 1

Learning biographies tend to be cumulative. Do you think such trends may be attenuated or even corrected? Explain and discuss your arguments.

Exercise 2

Life transitions tend to be intensive phases in people's educational life course. Give a few examples and explain this phenomenon.

Task

Alheit and Dausien (2002) use the concept of biographicity to renew, enlarge, and deepen the notion of lifelong learning. Refer to their article in order to clarify the "double face" of LLL and to discover how making reference to biographicity helps to clarify this ambiguity.

Alheit, P. & Dausien, B. (2002). The double face of lifelong learning: Two analytical perspectives on a 'silent revolution'. *Studies in the Education of Adults* 34, 3-22.

8.3 A comprehensive attempt

A comprehensive sociological analysis of adult learning participation needs to encompass the various factors noted above. It also has to include the role and function of adult learning in society and, finally, to articulate these various dimensions in theoretical terms.

Participation in adult learning activities results from an ongoing tension between people's learning aspirations, organisational demand, and the availability of learning opportunities. Sociologically, we could say that adult education participation takes place at the intersection of **learning demand** and **institutional response**, both of which have been socially constructed.

Learning demand is constructed out of the functional imperative of society or of organisations and out of individuals' cultural dispositions and aspirations. Such social demand (see Figure 3) is always a social construct coming out of formal or informal mediation or negotiation between the requirements of an organisation or society and people's aspirations and perceived interests. Learning demand is a social demand because of the requirements of the social structure in which the individual evolves and because of individual aspirations that are greatly influenced by people's environment.

Figure 3: Learning demand

Source: Author's own

An organisation's external functional imperative is related to new or different capacities for action required of its members or staff, while subjective demand has to do with personal aspiration and expectation. Learning demand is always a dialectical reality because of the inevitable mediation taking place more or less overtly between these two components. At the workplace, external demand used to be met through external flexibility, i.e. through hiring and firing. Today, organisations tend to respond to growing demand through internal flexibility, i.e. through education and training. Such external demand is also determined by a firm's external context, by situational factors like firm size and industrial sectors, as well as by current adult learning policies in society.

Regarding the subjective component of the social demand for learning, an individual's inclination to engage in active learning in a period of changes needs to be understood, upstream, in terms of what goes on in the individual's mind when they decide to (or not to) mobilise their learning resources to master new knowledge or skills. Such a decision is heavily dependent on the subjective perception of active learning as a resource to manage a situation. Two dimensions are involved in this internal process: first, the individual's genuine belief that such learning will be useful for them in the given context and, second, their perception of their own ability to succeed in the intended learning exercise, i.e. a sense of educational efficiency.

According to Rubenson's **valence-expectancy theory** and its recruitment paradigm (Rubenson, 1977; Bergsten, 1980), the decision to participate in ALE (see Figure 4) is a combination of these two kinds of perception on the part of an individual: their assessment of the relevance or value of the intended activity (VALENCE) and their anticipation of being successful in this educational situation (EXPECTANCY). However, individual demand is, to a certain extent, also a social construct. The perception of being able to succeed (expectancy) is strongly influenced by past social and learning experiences, by earlier socialisation processes, by the information received, in short: by dispositional factors and the socio-economic circumstances of the people involved. Similarly, the positive, negative, or neutral valence ascribed to the proposed or intended learning activity is closely related to an individual's perception of their needs and their conviction that such learning will be useful, either because it is recognised by the respective milieu or because it helps improve capacities for action that the individual feels are necessary or beneficial in their life or work context. The concept of **learning press**, i.e. the extent to which a milieu fosters ALE participation, is often referred to in this context (Darkenwald & Merriam, 1982).

Figure 4: Valence-expectancy theory

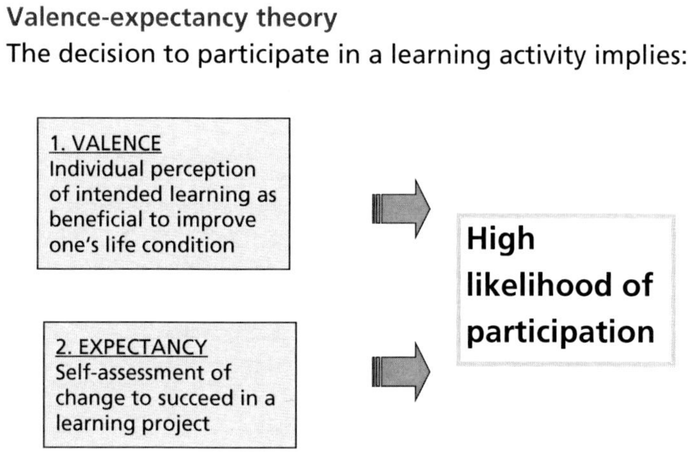

Source: Author's own.

The power of the perceived value of an educational activity (the valence) and of the likelihood of being able to participate in and/or benefit from it (expectancy) determines the intensity of an individual's motivation to participate either in externally required learning events or in a personal learning project. As Rubenson (1977, 1997) has shown, both of these motivational factors are in large parts socially conditioned. People's demand for acquiring new capacities for action in order to be able to pilot important shifts in their lives is constructed through accumulation of prior learning experiences, either positive or negative. Hence the paramount importance of policies supporting "expression and mediation of learning demand".

Exercises and Tasks

Exercise 1

Could you give examples of a potential ALE participant's perceptions of valence and expectancy?

Exercise 2

What factors could affect an individual's expectancy perception in positive ways?

Exercise 3

How do the two dimensions of learning demand come into play at the workplace, and how could they be mediated?

Exercise 4

Looking at the data in Table 12, how could we explain the differences in participation rates between small and large enterprises by referring to the relation between **learning demand** and **institutional response**?

Exercise 5

What link do you see between expectancy-valence theory and cognitive theory, especially with regard to motivation in general and, more specifically, to Bandura and Mezirow?

Task

Bergsten (1980) used Rubenson's expectancy-valence theory to better understand why people in Sweden, especially those with low levels of prior formal education, participate in adult education at lower rates than might be desired. Why and how do a person's perceptions related to work and/or leisure roles influence their participation in adult learning activities?
See Bergsten article:

Bergsten, U. (1980). Interest in education among adults with short previous formal schooling. *Adult Education Quarterly, 30*, 131-151.
http://aeq.sagepub.com/content/30/3/131.full.pdf+html

9. Conclusion on Participation Theories

Comparative data illustrate common trends across countries. Inequalities in ALE participation may be observed across countries with respect to similar factors such as formal schooling, level of qualification, age, and work context. These similarities notwithstanding, the fact that the degree of disparity differs between countries indicates that public policy and support can make a significant difference (Rubenson & Desjardins, 2009) by regulating the prevailing market logic.

Observed participation patterns and changing trends over time and across countries indeed result from a moving tension between social learning demands, in both their external and subjective components, and the availability of learning opportunities or responses (i.e. their accessibility, visibility, and flexibility). Both social learning demands and learning opportunities are socially constructed through various dispositional, institutional, and socio-economic factors.

10. General Conclusion

This publication on learning theories and theories of adult learning participation sought to address a wide range of questions. Inquiring into the meaning of adult learning, we reviewed the various theories of learning, asking what goes on when one acquires or mobilises new knowledge and skills. What does it mean to learn? What is the significance of past experiences and of informal learning? How do we assess the various roles of facilitators, trainers, or mentors? How do different environments influence learning aspirations and learning processes?

Based on a sociological analysis of adult education participation, we then observed participation patterns in their relation to socio-economic conditions and the extent of their social reproduction along life courses and across generations. Observing socially less predictable participation patterns has given us opportunities for assessing the relativity of social reproduction and for identifying the key conditions and variables that need to be addressed in order to alter prevailing trends. We outlined remedial policies that could make a difference.

The frequency of socially atypical participation patterns lead us to look at other forces driving people's learning biographies. Biographical analysis brought us back to a review of recent learning theorists with respect to the significance and impact of people's past experiences and of informal learning in transition phases. Individuals, in the social context of late modernity, have no choice but to pilot their numerous life transitions and to mobilise learning resources in actively embracing uncertainty.

An important dimension that has emerged from our review of theories is the ambiguity, and hence the potential and dynamics, that is always at work between social determination and individual initiatives, between individuals and their environment (Merriam & Cafarella, 1999). People's perception of usefulness of a given learning project (its valence) and their expectancy are in part socially determined, but may be also influenced and modified.

If the functional imperative of the social structure has a strong impact on the expression of learning demand, this demand is also inevitably influenced by the subjective aspiration of individuals who could negotiate or at least resist. Learning, a social and yet intimate activity, requires subjective involvement, which is too essential not to create space or at least interstice for modifying socially established perception or behaviour.

Antikainen (1998, p. 215) has phrased the question that runs through this publication quite well when he asked: "Assuming that we are moving towards an era of lifelong learning, what does this mean at the level of individual life?" And what does it mean at the level of local and global governance, I would like to add, if we want individuals and societies to actively confront today's economic, environmental, and social challenges? The issue is not only making learning resources more accessible, but also creating conditions to sustain meaningful and transformative learning experiences. This issue is to create spaces and support for people to be able to mobilise the learning resources required in the ongoing construction of their life course and in the development of their communities. The issue is to curb the prevalent imbalanced trends in adult education participation: social imbalance in terms of participants' social profiles and economicist imbalance in terms of the availability of learning resources in the various areas of human activity.

Learning is not a passive act of reception through which an individual is assimilated into institutionalised values and norms. Learning is certainly a socialisation process through which citizens integrate the rules of the game, yet the *game of their life* is far from being settled in advance! Learners may and do, in some contexts, personally articulate the internalisation and appropriation of values, norms, and knowledge. Learners may resist socialisation. They may even create new values or counter orientations. Within the frame of larger social movements, people may dispute part of the school curriculum and may argue to that effect with teachers or tutors. Employees may challenge the orientation of health and safety programmes offered by their employers. A patient may, through other sources, counter-check the diagnosis made by learned medical doctors. Workers can express their own learning aspiration or expectancy and require mediation between the organisation's request and their demand.

Learners are emotional and rational subjects eager and able to co-pilot their biographies. Again, learning is both a socialisation process and the inner driven construction of one-self. This built-in tension is what makes the social recognition of the intimacy of learning a critical issue in late modernity. The dynamics of adult learning are dialectical, and therefore the notion of the intimacy of learning underlines the ambiguity, in any learning demand, between the functional requirement of society and the lifelong aspiration of individuals to develop themselves intellectually and construct their own identity.

This emerging interest for the intimacy of learning is not an isolated phenomenon in adult learning today. Its emergence is related to recent trends reminding us of the subjectivity of learning lives. The rediscovery and validation of informal learning and the growing insistence on self-learning, on sense of self-efficiency, on reflective practice in experiential learning and on atypical patterns of participation are converging trends showing the distinctive character of learning biographies. The intimate experience of learning is where subjects build their idiosyncrasy. It is through active reference to past experience that the subject makes learning "significant" and thus operative. Of course, individuals are deeply influenced by their environment and social structure, but they can and do resist; they can alter their social and physical environment or transit to another one. If it is true that social, institutional, and cultural factors influence participation, it is also true that people may find ways to participate and strive to modify or articulate prevailing factors or conditions.

In the workplace, for example, the recognition of the intimacy of learning is transforming the learning demand. On the one hand, individuals insist on having a say in their personal and professional development and, on the other, organisations are increasingly recognising the personal commitment of learners as a precondition not only for successfully acquiring and transferring skills and knowledge, but also for developing a capacity for initiative, a crucial late modern competency.

The recognition of the intimacy of learning is an important social issue because of the social consequences of neglecting this critical dimension for ensuring significant and transformative learning. It is a social issue also because of the complexities of the current life course dynamics. The need for social recognition of the intimate dimension of the learning process resonates with a larger social transformation in late modernity. Indeed, life course uncertainties, plurality of ideological frames of reference and growing risks in both the environment and the social life make it so that individuals repeatedly find themselves in new contexts where they have to continuously negotiate life crossroads and manage transitions. "Living a life is becoming more and more problematic and unpredictable" (Antikainen, 1998, p. 116).

At the end of this expedition, we may have more queries about the complexity of learning lives than at the beginning. If this is true, if our theoretical curiosity has been tickled, the main goal of this book has been accomplished.

References

Aldridge, F. & Tuckett, A. (2007). *The road to nowhere? The NIACE survey on adult participation in learning*. Leicester: NIACE.

Alheit, P. & Dausien, B. (2002). The double face of lifelong learning: Two analytical perspectives on a 'silent revolution'. *Studies in the Education of Adults* 34, 3-22.

Alheit, A. (1994). The biographical question as a challenge to adult education. *International Education Review*, 40, 283-298.

Alheit, P. & Dausien, B. (1999). *'Biographicity' as a basic resource of lifelong learning*. Presented at the European Conference, University of Bremen.

Alheit, P., Bron-Wojciechowska, A., Brugger, E. & Dominicé, P. (1995). *The biographical approach in European adult education*. Vienna: Edition Volkshochschule, 107-119.

Allal, L. (1998). *Processus et difficultés d'apprentissage*. Genève: Université de Genève.

Antikainen, A. (1998).Between structure and subjectivity: Life histories and lifelong learning. International Review of Education, 44, (2-3):215-234.

Antikainen, A. & Juha, K. (2002). Educational generations and the futures of adult education: A Nordic experience. *International Journal of Lifelong Education*, 21, 209-219.

Astolfi, J. P. (1997). *L'erreur, un outil our enseigner*. Paris: ESF Editeur.

Bandura, A. (1977). *Social learning theory*. Englewood Cliffs, NJ: Prenctice-Hall. Inc.

Bandura, A. (1989). Social cognitive theory. In R. Vasta (Ed.), *Annals of child development. Vol.6: Six theories of child development* (pp. 1-60). Greenwich, CT: JAI Press.

Bandura, A. (1994). Self-efficacy. In V. S. Ramachaudran (Ed.), *Encyclopedia of human behavior, Volume 4* (pp. 71-81). New York: Academic Press

Beard, C. & Wilson, J. (2006). *Experiential learning: A best practice handbook for educators and trainers*. (2nd edition). London/Philadelphia: Kogan Page.

Beck, U. & Beck-Gernsheim, E. (2002). *Individualization*. London: Sage Publications.

Beck, U. (1992). *Risk Society: Towards a new modernity*. London: Sage publications.

Bélanger, P. & Tuijnman, A. (Eds.). (1997). *New patterns for adult learning: A six-country comparative study*. London: Pergamon Press.

Bélanger, P. & Valdivielso, S. (Eds.) (1997). *The emergence of learning societies: Who participates in adult learning?* London: Pergamon Press.

Bélanger, P., Doray, P., Labonté, A. & Levesque, M. (2005). *Les participations atypiques: des exceptions qui indiquent de nouvelles voies*. Montréal: CIRDEP-CIRSST, UQAM et Québec: MESSF.

Bergsten, U. (1980). Interest in education among adults with short previous formal schooling. *Adult Education*, 30, 131-151.

Blair, A., McPake, J. & Munn, P. (1995). A new conceptualisation of adult participation in education. *British Educational Research Journal*, 21, 629-644.

Boateng, S.K. (2009). Significant country differences in adult learning. *Eurostats, Statistics in Focus*, 44/2009.

Bourdieu P. & Passeron, J.-C. (1970). *La reproduction*. Paris : Éditions de Minuit.

Bowl, M. (2001). Experiencing the barriers: Non-traditional students entering higher education. *Research Papers in Education*, 16, 141-160.

Bruner, J. (2009). Culture, mind and education. In K. Illeris (Ed.), *Contemporary theories of learning* (pp. 159-168). London: Routledge.

Bruner, J., Goodnow, J. & Austin, G. (1956*). A study of thinking*. New York: Wiley.

Bruner, J. (1996). *The culture of education*, Harvard University Press, Cambridge.

Burpee, J. (2005). *Experiential learning theory: They didn't teach THAT in library school.* A Power Point presentation: Guelph: Library Peter Wolf, Teaching Support Services.

Cahalan, T. M. & Lacireno-Paquet, N. (1998). *Adult education participation decisions and barriers: Review of conceptual frameworks and empirical studies*. Washington: US Department of Education, Office of Educational Research and Improvement, National Centre for Education Statistics, Working Paper No. 98-10.

Chomsky, N. (1968). *Language and mind*, Harcourt, Brace, and World, New York

Colardyn, D. & Bjornavold, J. (2004) Validation of formal, non-formal and informal learning: Policy and practices in EU member states. *European Journal of Education*, 39(1), 69-89.

Cookson, P. (1986). A framework for theory and research on adult education participation. *Adult Education Quaterly*, 36(3), 130-141.

Cordova, D. I. & Lepper, M. R. (1996). Intrinsic motivation and the process of learning: Beneficial effects of contextualization, personalization, and choice. *Journal of Educational Psychology*, 88, 715–730.

Courtney, S. (1992) *Why adults learn: Towards a theory of participation in adult education*. London: Routledge.

Cross, K. P. (1982). *Adults as learners*. San Francisco: Jossey-Bass Publishers.

Crossan B., Field J., Gallacher J. & Merrill, B. (2003). Understanding participation in learning for non-traditional adult learners: Learning careers and the construction of learning identities. *British Journal of Sociology of Education*, 24, 55-67.

Darkenwald, G.D. & Merriam, S.B. (1982). *Adult education: Foundations of practice*. New York: Harper Collins.

Darkenwald, G.D. & Valentine, T. (1985). Factor structure of deterrents to public participation in adult education. *Adult Education Quarterly*, 35(4), 177-193.

De Montlibert, C. (1973). Le public de la formation des adultes. *Revue française de sociologie*, XIV, 529-545.

De Montlibert, C. (1997). L'éducation permanente et la promotion des classes moyennes. *Sociologie du travail*, 19(3), 243-265.

De Sanctis, F. (1988). *Verso un duemila educativo*. Prato: Università degli studi di Firenze, Commune de Prato.

Desjardins, R., Rubenson, K. & Milana, M. (2006). *Unequal chances to participate in adult learning: International perspectives*. Paris: UNESCO-IIEP. Retrieved from http://unesdoc.unesco.org

Dewey, J. (1940). *Education today*. New York: Greenwood Press, Publishers.

Dominicé, P. (1990). *L'histoire de vie comme processus de formation*. Paris: L'Harmattan.

Doray, P., Bélanger, P. & Labonté, A. (2005). *Les contours de la demande insatisfaite de formation*. Note de recherche n° 5. Montréal : CIRDEP-CIRST/UQAM et Québec: MESSF.

Doray, P., Bélanger, P., Motte, A. & Labonté, A. (2005). *Les facteurs de variation de la participation des adultes à la formation au Canada en 1997*. Montréal: CIRDEP-CIRSST-UQAM et Québec: MSSF

Erickson, D. (2007). A developmental re-forming of the phases of meaning in transformational learning. *Adult Education Quarterly*, 58, 61-80.

Evans, N. (Ed.) (2000). *Experiential learning around the world*. London: Jessica Kingsley Publishers.

Fagan, W. T. (1988). Concepts of reading and writing among low-literate adults. *Reading Research and Instructions*, 27, 47-60.

Fosnot, C. T. (2005). Constructivism revisited: Implications and reflections. In C.T. Fosnot (Ed.), *Constructivism: Theory, perspectives, and practice* (pp. 276-291). New York: Teachers College Press.

Freire, P. (1970). *Pedagogy of the oppressed*. New York: Herder and Herder.

Gagné, R. (1985). *The conditions of learning and theory of instruction* (4th edition). New York: CBS College Publishing.

Gallacher, J., Field, J., Merrill, B. & Crossan, B. (2002). Learning careers and the social space: Exploring the fragile identities of adult returners in the new further education. *International Journal of Lifelong Education*, 21, 493-509.

Gerard, H. (1992). Dissonance theory: A cognitive psychology with an engine. *Psychological Inquiry*, 3, 323-327.

Gorard, S.-R.-G., Renold, E. & Fevre, R. (1998). *Family influences on participation in lifelong learning*, Working paper 15. Cardiff: School of Education, Cardiff University.

Hédoux, J. (1982). Des publics et des «non-publics» de la formation des adultes. *Revue française de sociologie*, 23, 253-274.

Henry, G.T. & Basile, K.C. (1994) Understanding the decision to participate in formal adult education. *Adult Education Quarterly*, 44(2), 64-82.

Illeris, K. (2004). *Adult education and adult learning*. Copenhagen: Roskilde University Press and Malabar, FL: Krieger Publishing.

Illeris, K. (Ed.). (2009). *Contemporary theories of learning*. London: Routledge.

Illeris, K. (2003). Learning Changes through Life. *Lifelong Learning in Europe*, 8, 51-60.
Jarvis, P. (2009). Learning to be a person in society. In K. Illeris (Ed.), *Contemporary theories of learning* (pp. 21-34). London: Routledge.
Johnstone, J.W. & Rivera, R. J. (1965). *Volunteers for learning*. Chicago: Aldine Publishing Co.
Kegan, R. (2000). What "forms" transforms? A constructivism-development approach to transformative learning. In J. Mezirow (Ed.), *Learning as transformation*. (pp. 35-70) San Franscisco: Jossey-Bass.
King, P. & Kitchener, K. (1994). *Developing reflective judgment*. San Franscisco: Jossey-Bass.
Knowles, M. (1990). *The adult learner, a neglected species* (4th edition). Houston: Gulf Publishing.
Kolb, D. A., Boyatzis, R. & Mainemelis, C. (2001). Experiential learning theory: Previous research and new directions. In R.J. Sternberg & L.F. Zhang, L. (Eds.), *Perspectives on thinking, learning, and cognitive styles* (pp. 227–247). Mahwah, NJ: Lawrence Erlbaum.
Kolb, D.A. (1984). *Experiential learning: Experience as the source of learning and development*. Englewoods Cliffs: N.J.: Prenctice Hall.
Lave, J. (1988). *Cognition in practice*. New York: Cambridge University Press.
Lave, J. (1993). The practice of learning. In S. Chaiklin & J. Lave (Eds.), *Understanding practice: Perspectives on activity and context* (pp. 3-32). Cambridge, UK Cambridge University Press.
Lave, J. & Wenger, E. (1991). *Situated learning: Legitimate peripheral participation*. Cambridge: Cambridge University Press.
Legendre, R. (2005). *Dictionnaire actuel de l'éducation*. 3ème édition. Montréal: Guérin.
Leonard, D. (2002). *Learning theories A to Z*. London: Greenwood Press.
Livingstone, D.W. (2002). *Mapping the iceberg*. Toronto: NALL Working Paper n° 54.
Macedo, D. (Ed.). (2000). *Chomsky on mis-education*. New York: Rowman & Littlefield Publishers Inc.
Maslow, A. (1970). *Motivation and personality* (2nd ed.). New York: Harper-Collins.
Merriam, S. & Caffarella, R. (1999). *Learning in adulthood. A comprehensive guide* (2nd ed.). San Francisco: Jossey-Bass.
Mezirow, J. (1991). *Transformative dimensions of adult learning*. San Francisco: Jossey-Bass.
Mezirow, J. (1994). Understanding tranformation theory. *Adult Education Quarterly*, 44, 222-232.
Mezirow, J. (1996). Contemporary paradigms of learning. *Adult Education Quarterly*, 46, 158-173.
Mezirow, J. (2003). Transformative learning as discourse. *Journal of Transformative Education*, 1, 58-63.
Mezirow, J. (2006). An overview o transformative learning. In P. Sutherland & J. Crowther (Eds.), *Lifelong learning: Concepts and contexts*. (pp. 24-38) London: Routledge.

Schuller, T. & Watson, D., 2009, *Learning through life: Inquiry into the future for lifelong learning* (IFLL), Leicester,U.K.: NIACE.

Peters, V. (2004). *Working and training: First results of the 2003 Adult Education and Training Survey.* Culture, Tourism and the Centre for Education Statistics Research papers series. Ottawa: Statistics Canada Catalogue number 81-595-MIE20040015.

Piaget, J. (1964). Development and learning. *Journal of Research in Science Teaching*, 2,176-186.

Quigley, A. B. & Arrowsmith, S. (1997). The non-participation of undereducated adults. In P. Bélanger and A. Tuijnman (Eds.), *New patterns of adult learning: A six country comparative study* (pp. 101-130). London: Pergamon Press.

Reay, D., Ball, S.J. & David, M. (2002). It's taking me a long time but I'll get there in the end: Mature students on access courses and higher education service. *British Educational Research Journal*, 28, 5-19.

Rogers, C. (1969). *Freedom to learn.* Columbus, Ohio: Charles E. Merrill.

Rogers, C.R. (1979). *The foundations of the person-centred approach.* Education, 100, 96–107.

Rubenson K. (2003). Adult education and cohesion. *Lifelong Learning in Europe*, 8, 23-31.

Rubenson, K. & Xu, G. (1997). Barriers to participation in adult education and training: Towards a new understanding. In P. Bélanger and A. Tuijnman (Eds.), *New patterns for adult learning: A six-country comparative study* (pp. 77-100). London: Pergamon Press.

Rubenson, K. & Desjardins, R. (2009). The impact of welfare state regimes on barriers to participation in adult education. *Adult Education Quarterly*, 59 (3), 187-207.

Scanlan, C.S. & Darkenwald, G. D. (1984). Identifying deterrents to participation in continuing education. *Adult Education Quarterly*, 34(3), 155-166.

Schön, D. A. (1983). *The reflective practitioner.* New York: Basic Books.

Silberman, M. (2007). *The handbook of experiential learning.* San Francisco: Pfeiffer.

Silva, T., Cahalan, M. & Lacireno-Paquet, N. (1998). Adult education participation decisions and barriers: Review of conceptual frameworks and empirical studies. Washington: NCES.

Skinner, B. F. (1953). *Science and human behavior.* New York: Macmillan.

Skinner, B. F. (1974). *About behaviorism.* New York: Knopf.

Statistics Canada. (2003). *International adult literacy and life skills survey.* Ottawa: Statistics Canada. Retrieved from http://www.statcan.gc.ca.

Sternberg R. J. & Zhang L. F. (Eds.). (2000). *Perspectives on cognitive, learning, and thinking styles.* Mahwah, NJ: Lawrence Erlbaum.

Sutherland, P. & Crowther, J. (2006). *Lifelong learning: Concepts and contexts.* London: Routledge.

Thorndike, E. L. (1931). *Human learning.* Century: New York.

Thorndike, E. L. (1932). *The fundamentals of learning.* New York: Teachers College Press.

Tinto, V. (1993). *Leaving colleges: Rethinking the causes and cures of student attrition*. Chicago: Chicago University Press.

TNS Infratest. (2008). *Weiterbildungbeteiligung in Deutschland: Eckdaten zum BSW-AES 2007*. Munich: TNS Infratest.

Von Rosenbladt, B. & Bilger, F. (2008). *Weiterbildungsverhalten in Deutschland.* Bonn: DIE.

Watson, J. B. (1930). *Behaviorism*. Chicago: University of Chicago Press.

Wenger, E. (1998). *Communities of practice: Learning, meaning and identity*. Cambridge, MA: Harvard University Press.

Wikelund, K.R., Reder, S. & Hart-Landsberg, S. (1992). *Expanding theories of adult literacy participation: A literature review*. Philadelphia: University of Pennsylvania, National Centre on Adult Literacy, Technical Report TR 92-1.

About the Author

Paul Bélanger is currently a professor of education at the Université du Quèbec in Montréal (Canada) and the director of the Interdisciplinary Research Centre on Lifelong Learning (CIRDEP). Since 2009, he has also served as director of the Observatory on work related adult learning policies. Furthermore, he is a guest professor at the European Master in Adult Education programme in Essen (Germany). From 1989 to 2000, he was the director of the UNESCO Institute for Education in Hamburg (Germany), now known as the UNESCO Institute for Lifelong Learning.

Paul Bélanger has contributed to the field through scientific publications in books, journals, and encyclopedia entries, including: *Lifelong learning* (Kluwer, 1995), *Shifting patterns in adult education participation* (Pergamon, 1997), *Transitions toward LLL: Social indicators* (Tokyo, 1998), *Unlocking peoples' creative forces: A transnational Analysis of adult learning policies* (UNESCO 2000), "Learning Cities, Concept and Issues" in Duke, et al. 2006, *Making Knowledge Work*, NIACE). *Portrait of work-related learning in Quebec* (Ottawa 2008: CCL/ WLKC).

In 2000, Paul Bélanger was elected president of the International Council for Adult Education (ICAE). This UN-recognised international NGO on adult education is based in Montevideo (Uruguay); it draws together six regional bureaus (Africa, Asia, Latin America, Europe, Arab states, and the Caribbean) along with more than 170 national members.

Index